Plutarch: Concerning The Mysteries Of Isis And Osiris

G. R. S. Mead

Kessinger Publishing's Rare Reprints

Thousands of Scarce and Hard-to-Find Books on These and other Subjects!

- Americana
- Ancient Mysteries
- Animals
- Anthropology
- Architecture
- Arts
- Astrology
- Bibliographies
- Biographies & Memoirs
- Body, Mind & Spirit
- Business & Investing
- Children & Young Adult
- Collectibles
- Comparative Religions
- Crafts & Hobbies
- Earth Sciences
- Education
- Ephemera
- Fiction
- Folklore
- Geography
- Health & Diet
- History
- Hobbies & Leisure
- Humor
- Illustrated Books
- Language & Culture
- Law
- Life Sciences
- Literature
- Medicine & Pharmacy
- Metaphysical
- Music
- Mystery & Crime
- Mythology
- Natural History
- Outdoor & Nature
- Philosophy
- Poetry
- Political Science
- Science
- Psychiatry & Psychology
- Reference
- Religion & Spiritualism
- Rhetoric
- Sacred Books
- Science Fiction
- Science & Technology
- Self-Help
- Social Sciences
- Symbolism
- Theatre & Drama
- Theology
- Travel & Explorations
- War & Military
- Women
- Yoga
- *Plus Much More!*

**We kindly invite you to view our catalog list at:
http://www.kessinger.net**

THIS ARTICLE WAS EXTRACTED FROM THE BOOK:

Thrice Greatest Hermes Part 1

BY THIS AUTHOR:

G. R. S. Mead

ISBN 0766126129

READ MORE ABOUT THE BOOK AT OUR WEB SITE:

http://www.kessinger.net

OR ORDER THE COMPLETE
BOOK FROM YOUR FAVORITE STORE

ISBN 0766126129

IX

Plutarch: Concerning the Mysteries of Isis and Osiris

FOREWORD

IN the chapter on Philo we attempted to set before the reader some outlines of the central doctrine of Hellenistic theology—the sublime concept of the Logos—as envisaged by a learned Jew of the Diaspora, steeped in Hellenism, and living in the capital of Egypt and the centre of the intellectual life of Greater Greece.

In the present chapter we shall endeavour to give the reader a further insight into this master-idea from another standpoint, and shall reproduce the views of a learned Greek, who, while remaining on the ground of Hellenic traditions proper, turns his eyes to Egypt, and reads what part of its mysterious message he can decipher, in Greek modes of thought.

Plutarch, of Chæroneia in Bœotia, flourished in the second half of the first century A.D., and so follows immediately on Philo and on Paul; like Philo, however, he knows nothing of the Christians, though like the Alexandrian he treats of precisely those problems and questions which were and are of pre-eminent interest for Christians.

Plutarch chooses as his theme the myth and mysteries of Osiris and Isis. He gives the myth in its main outlines, and introduces us into the general religious atmosphere of the Egyptian belief of what we may, perhaps, be allowed to call "Demotic" times. But he does far more than this. Initiated himself into the Osiriaca, of which there was apparently a *thiasos* at Delphi, though on the one hand he possesses more knowledge of formal details than he feels himself permitted to disclose, on the other hand he is aware that the "true initiate of Isis" is one who goes far beyond any formal reception of the symbolic mysteries; the true initiate must of his own initiative for ever keep searching and probing more deeply into the intimate reason of things, as adumbrated by the "things said and done" in the sacred rites (iii, 3).

For this task Plutarch is well equipped, not only by his wide knowledge of the philosophy and theology and science of his day, but also by the fact that he held a high office at Delphi in the service

THE MYSTERIES OF ISIS AND OSIRIS

of Apollo and also in connection with the Dionysiac rites. He was almost certainly a hierophant, and no merely formal one at that.

Plutarch accordingly gives a most instructive exposition, which should enable us, if only we are content to put ourselves in his place, and condescend to think in the terms of the thought of his day, to review the ancient struggle between physical reason and formal theology which was then in full conflict—a conflict that has been renewed on a vastly extended scale for the last few centuries, and which is still being fought to a finish or honourable truce in our own day.

Our initiated philosopher is on the side neither of atheism or pure physicism, nor on that of superstition, as he understood those terms in his day; he takes a middle ground, and seeks final refuge in the fair vision of the Logos; and that, too, in all humility, for he knows well that whatever he can say is at best but a dim reflection of the glory of the Highest, as indeed he expressly tells us when writing:

"Nor can the souls of men here on the earth, swathed as they are in bodies and enwrapped in passions, commune with God, except so far as they can reach some dim sort of a dream of Him with the perception of a mind trained in philosophy" (lxxiii, 2).

We accordingly find Plutarch discussing the various theories of his day which professed to explain the mythological and theological enigmas of the ancients, with special reference to the Osiris myth.

He discusses the theory of Evemerus, that the gods were nothing but ancient kings and worthies, and dismisses it as no really satisfactory explanation (xxiii).

He then proceeds to consider the theory that these things refer to the doings of daimones—which he thinks a decided improvement on that of Evemerus (xxv).

Thence he passes to the theories of the Physicists or natural phenomenalists (xxxii), and of the Mathematici—that is to say, the Pythagorean speculations as to the celestial spheres, and their harmonies (xli).

In each of these three latter theories he thinks there is some truth; still each by itself is insufficient; they must be combined (xlv), and even then it is not enough.

He next considers the question of first principles, and discusses the theories of the One, the Two, and the Many; again finding something to be said for each view, and yet adopting none of them as all-sufficient.

But of all attempted interpretations he finds the least satisfactory to be that of those who are content to limit the hermeneutics of the mystery-myths simply to the operations of ploughing and sowing. With this "vegetation god" theory he has little patience, and stigmatises its professors as that "dull crowd" (lxv). And here, perhaps, some of us may think that Plutarch is not out of date even in the twentieth century of grace, and his arguments might be recommended to the consideration of those anthropologists who are just now with such complacency running to death what Mr Andrew Lang humorously calls the "Covent Garden" theory.

Further on, dealing as he does with the puzzling question of Egyptian "animal worship", Plutarch is brought face to face with many problems of "taboo" and "totemism", and he is not without interest in what he says on these subjects (lxxii, f.), and in the theories of utilitarianism and symbolism which he adduces (lxxiv).

Finally, he gives us his view of the *rationale* of the custom of incense-burning (lxxix), which should be of some concern to many in present-day Christian communities.

But the whole of this complex of custom and rites, puzzling and self-contradictory as they may appear, and the whole of the riddles and veiled enigmas of Egyptian priestly tradition, are, Plutarch believes, resolvable into transparent simplicity by a proper understanding of the true nature of man and of his relation to Divine Nature, that Wisdom who is the eternal and inseparable spouse of Divine Reason, the Logos.

It would perhaps have been simpler for some of my readers—it certainly would have been shorter—had I condensed what Plutarch has to say; but my desire is rather to let this student of the comparative theology of his day speak for himself, and not to give my own views; for I still believe, in spite of the superior formal education of the twentieth century, that we cannot normally know more about the ancient mysteries and their inner purport than the best minds who were initiated into them while they still flourished.

For not only are we without the precise data which these ancients possessed, but also the phase of thought through which we have recently been passing, and in which we mostly still are, is not one which can sympathetically tolerate those very considerations which, in my opinion, provide the most fertile ground of explanation of the true inwardness of what was best in those mystery-traditions.

Moreover, I have thought it of service to give a full version of this

THE MYSTERIES OF ISIS AND OSIRIS

treatise of Plutarch's from a decent critical text,[1] for the only translation in English read by me is by no means a careful piece of work,[2] and manifestly rendered from a very imperfect text; also, the language of Plutarch in some passages appears to me to be deserving of more careful handling than has as yet been accorded it, for a number of sentences seem to have been purposely phrased so as to be capable of conveying a double meaning.

Finally, with regard to his own interpretation, I would suggest that Plutarch, as was natural to a Greek, has more insisted on intellectual modes of thought than perhaps an Egyptian priest would have been inclined to do; for it seems probable that to the Egyptian mind the chief interest would lie in the possibility of the realisation of immediate contact with the Mystery in all those modes which are not so much intellectual as sensible; in other words, it would be by making himself a vehicle of the Great Breath in his body rather than a mirror of the Mystery in his mind, that the son of the Nile Land would seek for union.

It is, moreover, of interest to find that Plutarch addresses his treatise to a lady. For though we have extant several moral tractates addressed to wives—such as Porphyry's *Letter* to Marcella, and Plutarch's *Consolation* to his own wife, Timoxena—it is rare to find philosophical treatises addressed to women, and nowadays many women are once more interested in such "philosophy".

Plutarch wrote his essay at Delphi (lxviii, 6), and addressed it to Klea, a lady who held a distinguished position among the Delphic priestesses, and who had herself been initiated into the Osiriac Mysteries—her very name Klea being, perhaps, her mystery-name (xxxv). The treatise is, therefore, addressed to one who was prepared to read into it more than appears on the surface.

It should also be remembered that in all probability the main source of Plutarch's information was the now lost treatise of Manetho on the Egyptian Religion, and in this connection it is of interest to record Granger's opinion, who, in referring to Plutarch's *De Iside et Osiride*, says:

"First he deals with those opinions which identify the Egyptian

---

[1] I use the texts of Parthey, *Plutarch: Über Isis und Osiris* (Berlin, 1850), and of Bernardakis, *Plutarchi Chaeronensis Moralia* ("Bibliotheca Teubneriana"; Leipzig, 1889), ii, 471 ff.

[2] See King (C. W.), *Plutarch's Morals: Theosophical Essays* (London, 1889), pp. 1–71. S. Squire's *Plutarch's Treatise of Isis and Osiris* (Cambridge, 1744) I have not read, and few can procure a copy nowadays.

gods with natural objects—Osiris with the Nile, Isis with the land, and so on. Then he considers the interpretations of those who identify the gods with the sun and moon, etc. (ch. lxi). These speculations summarise for us, at first or second hand, some of the Hermetic books current in Plutarch's time."[1]

CONCERNING ISIS AND OSIRIS

ADDRESS TO KLEA CONCERNING GNOSIS AND THE SEARCH FOR TRUTH[2]

I. 1.[3] While all who have mind, O Klea, should ask for all their blessings from the Gods—let *us*, by pursuing after them, pray to obtain from them those [blessings] of gnosis[4] concerning them, as far as 'tis within the reach of men; in that there's nothing greater for a man to get, nor more majestic for a God to give, than Truth.

2. Of other things their God *gives* men what they require, whereas of mind and wisdom He *gives a share*[5] to them—since He [Himself] possesses these and uses [them].

For the Divine is neither blest through silver and through gold, nor strong through thunderings and lightnings, but [blest and strong] by gnosis and by wisdom.

3. And thus most finely of all things which he hath said about the Gods—sounding aloud:

Yea have they both a common source and one [fair] native land;
But Zeus came into being first and he knew more—

hath Homer made pronouncement of the primacy of Zeus as more majestic, in that in gnosis and in wisdom it[6] is older.

4. Nay, I believe that the good fortune of æonian life—the which the God hath gotten for his lot—is that by reason of His gnosis the things in genesis should not entirely die; for when the knowing of existing things and being wise is taken from it, freedom from death is Time—not Life.

---

[1] Granger (F.), "The Poemander of Hermes Trismegistus", *Jour. Theol. Stud.*, vol. v, No. 19, p. 399.
[2] I have added some sub-headings as an indication of contents.
[3] I have numbered the paragraphs for greater convenience of reference.
[4] ἐπιστήμης.
[5] A play on δίδωσιν and μετα-δίδωσιν.
[6] Sc. the primacy.

THE MYSTERIES OF ISIS AND OSIRIS

THE ART OF KNOWING AND OF DIVINISING

II. 1. Wherefore the longing for the Godly state is a desire for Truth, and specially the [truth] about the Gods, in so much as it doth embrace reception of the sacred [things]—instruction and research;[1] a work more holy than is all and every purging rite and temple-service, and not least pleasing to that Goddess whom thou servest, in that she is particularly wise and wisdom-loving, seeing her very name doth seem to indicate that knowing and that gnosis[2] is more suitable to her than any other title.

2. For that "Isis" is Greek,[3] and [so is] "Typhōn"—in that he's foe unto the Goddess, and is "puffed up"[4] through [his] unknowing and deceit, and tears the Holy Reason (*Logos*) into pieces and makes away with it; the which the Goddess gathers up again and recomposes, and transmits to those perfected in the art of divinising,[5]—which by the means of a continually sober life and by [their] abstinence from many foods and sexual indulgences, tempers intemperate pleasure-love, and doth accustom [them] to undergo, without being broken down, the rigorous tasks of service in the sacred [rites], the end of which is gnosis of the First and Lordly One, the One whom mind alone can know,[6] for whom the Goddess calls on [them] to seek, though He is by her side and one with her.

3. Nay more, the very appellation of the holy [place] doth plainly promise gnosis, that is *eidēsis*, of That-which-is; for it is named *Iseion*, as though "of them who *shall* know"[7] That-which-is, if that with reason (*logos*) and with purity[8] we enter in the holy [places] of the Goddess.

---

[1] τὴν μάθησιν ... καὶ ζήτησιν. Mathēsis was the technical Pythagorean term for gnosis.

[2] τὸ εἰδ-έναι καὶ τὴν ἐπ-ισ-τήμην—word-plays on Ἶσις.

[3] *Cf.* lx, 2. The Egyptian of Isis is Ast.

[4] τετυφωμένος—a play on τυφών—lit., "wrapped in smoke (τῦφος)", and because one so wrapped in smoke or clouds has his intelligence darkened, hence "puffed up with conceit", crazy and demented. Typhōn is the dark or hidden side of the Father.

[5] θειώσεως (not in L. and S. or Soph.); it presumably comes from the stem of θειόω, which means: (i) to smoke with sulphur and so purify; (ii) to make divine (θεῖος), and so transmute into godship. The sentence may thus also mean "those initiated into the sulphur rite"—a not impossible rendering when we remember the Alchemical literature which had its source in Chemia-Egypt. It will also permit us to connect brimstone with Typhōn—hoofs and all!

[6] Or the Intelligible—νοητοῦ.

[7] εἰς-ομένων τὸ ὄν—a play on ἰσ-εῖ-ον—fut. of √Ϝιδ (*vid*) from which comes also εἴδησις above. This may also mean "seeing" as well as "knowing", and thus may refer to the Epopteia or Mystery of Sight, and not the preliminary Mystery of Hearing (Muēsis).

[8] ὁσίως—another play on Ἶσις; *cf.* lx, 3.

THE TRUE INITIATES OF ISIS

III. 1. Yet many have set down that she is Hermes' daughter, and many [that she is] Prometheus's—holding the latter as discoverer of wisdom and foreknowledge, and Hermes of the art of letters and the Muses' art.

2. Wherefore, in Hermes-city, they call the foremost of the Muses Isis, as well as Righteousness,[1] in that she's wise,[2] as has been said,[3] and shows[4] the mysteries of the Gods to those who are with truth and justice called the Carriers of the holy [symbols] and Wearers of the holy robes.[5]

3. And these are they who carry the holy reason (*logos*) about the Gods, purged of all superstition and superfluity, in their soul, as in a chest, and cast robes round it[6]—in secret disclosing such [things] of the opinion[7] about the Gods as are black and shadowy, and such as are clear and bright, just as they are suggested by the [sacred] dress.

4. Wherefore when the initiates of Isis at their "death" are adorned in these [robes], it is a symbol that this Reason (*Logos*) is with them; and with Him and naught else they go there.[8]

5. For it is not the growing beard and wearing cloak that makes philosophers, O Klea, nor clothing in linen and shaving oneself that makes initiates of Isis; but a true Isiac is one who, when he by law[9] receives them, searches out by reason (*logos*) the [mysteries] shown and done concerning these Gods, and meditates upon the truth in them.

---

[1] δικαιοσύνην, or Justice (Maāt), that is, the "power of the Judge", Hermes being Judge of the Scales. The Nine are the Paut of Hermes, he being the tenth, the mystery being here read differently from the Ogdoad point of view—that is to say, macrocosmically instead of cosmically.

[2] Or, perhaps, the reading should be "Wisdom".

[3] *Cf.* ii, 1.

[4] δεικνύουσαν—probably a play on δικαιοσύνην.

[5] ἱεροφόροις καὶ ἱεροστόλοις. Plutarch by his "with truth and justice" warns the reader against taking these words to mean simply the carriers of the sacred vessels and instruments in the public processions, and the sacristans or keepers of the sacred vestments.

[6] περιστέλλοντες, which also means *componere*—that is, to lay out a corpse and so to bury.

[7] οἰήσεως = δόξης, appearance, seeming—that is, the public myth; as opposed to λόγος = ἐπιστήμη, knowledge or reality.

[8] Or "walk there"—that is, in "Hades". Or, again, the "death" is the death unto sin when they become Alive and walk among the "dead" or ordinary men.

[9] That is, when the initiation is a lawful one, or really takes effect; when a man's karma permits it, that is, after passing the proper tests.

THE MYSTERIES OF ISIS AND OSIRIS

WHY THE PRIESTS ARE SHAVEN AND WEAR LINEN

IV. 1. Now, as far as the "many" are concerned, even this commonest and smallest [secret] is hid from them,—namely, why the priests cut off their hair, and wear linen robes; for some do not at all care to know about these things, while others say that they abstain from [the use of] the sheep's wool, as they do from its flesh, because they hold it sacred, and that they shave their heads through being in mourning, and wear linen things on account of the colour which the flax in flower sends forth, resembling the ætherial radiance[1] that surrounds the cosmos.

2. But the true cause, [the] one of all, is, as Plato says, [because]: "It is not lawful for pure to touch not pure."[2]

Now, superfluity[3] of nourishment and excretion is nothing chaste or pure; and it is from superfluities that wool and fur and hair and nails spring up and grow.

3. It would, thus, be laughable for them to cut off their own hair in the purifications, shaving themselves, and making smooth their whole body evenly, and [then] put on and wear the [hair] of animals.[4]

4. For indeed we should think that Hesiod, when he says:

> Nor from five-branched at fire-blooming of Gods
> Cut dry from green with flashing blade[5]—

teaches that [men] ought to keep holy day only when pure of such [superfluities], and not at the sacred operations themselves have need of purification and the removal of superfluities.

---

[1] χρόαν—also meaning surface, skin, and tone in melody.   [2] *Phæd.*, 67 B.

[3] περίσσωμα—also probably here a play on that which is "round the body" (περὶ σῶμα)—namely, the hair.

[4] θρεμμάτων—lit., "things nourished" (from τρέφω), presumably a play on the "nourishment" (τροφή) above.

[5] *Op. et Dies*, 741 f. This scrap of ancient gnomic wisdom Hesiod has preserved, I believe, from the "Orphic" fragments still in circulation in his day in Bœotia among the people from an Older Greece. I have endeavoured to translate it according to the most primitive meaning of the words. In later days it was thought that "five-branched" was the hand, and that the couplet referred to a prohibition against paring the nails at a feast of the Gods! In this sense also Plutarch partly uses it. But if I am right in my version, we have in the lines a link with that very early tradition in Greece which in later times was revived by the Later Platonic School, in a renewed contact with the ancient Chaldæan mystery-tradition of the Fire. "Five-branched" would thus mean man, or rather purified man, and the saying referred to the "pruning of this tree". In it also we have an example of a "Pythagorean symbol" three hundred years before Pythagoras. Finally, I would remind the reader of the Saying which the Master is said to have uttered as He passed to the Passion of the Crucifixion (Luke xxiii, 31): "For if they do these things in the moist stock [A.V. green tree], what shall be done in the dry?"—presumably the quotation of an old gnomic saying or mystery *logos*. The "moist nature" is the feminine side of the "fiery" or "dry".

5. Again, the flax grows out of the deathless earth, and yields a fruit that man may eat, and offers him a smooth pure raiment that does not weigh upon the watcher,[1] but is well joined for every hour,[2] and is the least cone-bearing,[3] as they say—concerning which things there is another reason (*logos*).

OF THE REFRAINING FROM FLESH AND SALT AND SUPERFLUITIES

V. 1. And the priests handle so hardly[4] the nature of superfluities, that they not only deprecate the many kinds of pulse, and of meats the sheep-flesh[5] kinds and swine-flesh kinds, as making much superfluity, but also at their times of purification they remove the salts from the grains,[6] having other further reasons as well as the fact that it makes the more thirsty and more hungry sharpen their desire the more.

2. For to argue that salts are not pure owing to the multitude of small lives[7] that are caught[8] and die in them when they solidify themselves, as Aristagoras said,[9] is naïve.

3. They are, moreover, said to water the Apis also from a special well, and by all means to keep him from the Nile—not that they think His[10] water stained with blood because of the Crocodile,[11] as some think (for nothing is so precious to Egyptians as the Nile), but that the water of Nile's superfluity[12] on being drunk seems to make fat, nay, rather to make much too much of flesh.

---

[1] Reading σκοποῦντι for σκέποντι—that is, the soul.

[2] εὐάρμοστον δὲ πρὸς πᾶσαν ὥραν—"well adapted for every season" is the common translation; the "hour", however, is a technical astrological term.

[3] *Vulg.*, "lice-producing"—but φθείρ also means a special kind of pine producing small cones; and the great cone was a symbol of the Logos, and the small cone of physical generation. It is also connected with φθείρω, meaning to corrupt, and so to breed corruption.

[4] *Vulg.*, "endure with such difficulty" or "feel such disgust at".

[5] Referring usually to small animals of the sheep and goat kind, and more generally to all sacrificial animals.

[6] Or, perhaps, more generally, "the salt from their food". It more probably refers to mineral and not to vegetable salts.

[7] That is *animalculæ*.

[8] ἁλισκόμενα—probably a word-play on ἅλας (salts).

[9] Müller, ii, 99. Aristagoras was a Greek writer on Egypt, who flourished about the last quarter of the fourth century B.C.

[10] Namely the Nile, as Osiris, or the Great Deep.

[11] Mystically the "Leviathan" (*e.g.* of the "Ophites") who lived in the Great Deep. *Cf.* also Ps. civ, 26, where, speaking of the Great Sea (25), it is written: "There go the ships [the *barides*, boats, or vehicles of souls], and there is that Leviathan [LXX Dragon] whom thou hast fashioned to take his pastime [LXX sport or mock] therein."

[12] τὸ Νειλῷον ὕδωρ—τὰ Νειλῷα was the Feast of the Overflowing of the Nile.

THE MYSTERIES OF ISIS AND OSIRIS

4. And [so] they do not wish the Apis to be so nor yet themselves, but [wish] to wear their bodies on their souls compact and light, and neither to com-press nor op-press them by the mortal part prevailing and its weighing down of the divine.

ON THE DRINKING OF WINE

VI. 1. And as for wine, the servants of the God in Sun-city[1] do not at all bring it into the sacred place, as 'tis not right [for them] to drink by day while He, their Lord and King, looks on.

2. The rest [of them][2] use it indeed, but sparingly.

They have, however, many times of abstinence at which they drink no wine, but spend them in the search for wisdom, learning and teaching the [truth] about the Gods.

3. The kings used to drink it, though in certain measure according to the sacred writings, as Hecatæus has narrated,[3] for they were priests [as well].

4. They began to drink it, however, only from the time of Psammetichus;[4] but before that they used not to drink wine.

Nor did they make libation of it as a thing dear to the Gods, but as the blood of those who fought against the Gods[5]—from whom, when they fell and mingled with the earth, they think the vines came, and that because of this wine-drenching makes men to be out of their minds and struck aside,[6] in that, forsooth, they are full-filled with the forefathers of its[7] blood.[8]

5. These things, at any rate Eudoxus says, in Book II of his *Circuit*,[9] are thus stated by the priests.

ON FISH TABOOS

VII. 1. As to sea-fish, all [Egyptians] abstain generally (not from all [fish] but) from some; as, for example, those of the Oxyrhynchus

---

[1] Heliopolis—the God being the "Sun".

[2] *Sc.* the priests.

[3] Müller, ii, 389. H. flourished last quarter of sixth and first quarter fifth century B.C.

[4] Reigned 671–617 B.C.

[5] *Sc.* the Titans or Daimones as opposed to the Gods.

[6] Or "de-ranged"—παραπλῆγας. Paraplēx is the first of the daimonian rulers in *The Books of the Saviour* (*Pistis Sophia*, 367).

[7] *Sc.* the vine's.

[8] Or "with the blood of its forefathers".

[9] Or *Orbit*. Eudoxus flourished about the middle of the fourth century B.C.; he was initiated into the Egyptian mysteries, and a great astronomer, obtaining his knowledge of the art from the priests of Isis.

nome from those caught with a hook, for as they venerate the sharp-snouted fish,[1] they fear that the hook[2] is not pure when "sharp-snout" is caught by it;[3] while those of the Syēnē nome [abstain from] the "devourer",[4] for that it seems that it appears together with the rising of the Nile, and that it shows their[5] growth to those in joy, seen as a self-sent messenger.

2. Their priests, upon the other hand, abstain from all; and [even] on the ninth of the first month,[6] when every one of the rest of the Egyptians eats a broiled fish before his front door,[7] the priests do not taste it, but burn *their* fishes to ashes before the doors [of the Temple].[8]

3. And they have two reasons [for this], of which I will later on take up the sacred and extraordinary [one], according with the facts religiously deduced concerning Osiris and Typhon. The evident, the one that's close at hand, in showing forth the fish as a not necessary and a not unsuperfluous cooked food, bears witness unto Homer, who makes neither the Phæacians of luxurious lives, nor yet the Ithakēsian Island men, use fish, nor yet Odysseus's Companions[9] in so great a Voyage and on the Sea before they came to the last Strait.[10]

4. And generally [the priests] think that the sea's from fire and is beyond the boundaries—nor part nor element [of earth], but of another kind, a superfluity cor-rupted and cor-rupting.

THE ONION AND PIG TABOOS

VIII. 1. For nothing reasonless, or [purely] fabulous, or from [mere] superstition, as some suppose, has been incorporated into the

---

[1] τὸν ὀξύρυγχον—perhaps the pike.

[2] ἄγκιστρόν—dim. of ἄγκος, meaning a "bend" of any kind. Perhaps it may be intended as a play on the *ankh* tie or "noose of life", the well-known Egyptian symbol, generally called the *crux ansata*.

[3] If we read αὑτῷ for αὐτῷ it would suggest a mystic meaning, namely, "falls into his own snare".

[4] φαγροῦ—*Vulg.*, sea-bream; but Hesychius spells it φάγωρος, connecting it with φαγεῖν, to devour.

[5] Or "his" (the Nile's); but the "self-sent messenger" (αὐτάγγελος) seems to demand "their", and so suggests a mystical sense.

[6] Copt. Thoth—corr. roughly with September.

[7] πρὸ τῆς αὐλείου θύρας—that is, the outside door into the αὐλή, or court of the house. *Cf.* the title of the Trismegistic treatise given by Zosimus—"The Inner Door". There may, perhaps, be some mystical connection.

[8] *Cf.* Luke xxiv, 42: "And they gave Him a piece of broiled fish." This was *after* His "resurrection". Also *cf. Talmud Bab.*, "Sanhedrin", 103*a*: "That thou shalt not have a son or disciple who burns his food publicly, like Jeschu ha-Notzri" (D. J. L., 189).

[9] Compare the Companions of Horus in the Solar Boat.

[10] I fancy there must be some under-meaning here, and so I have put the key-words in capitals.

THE MYSTERIES OF ISIS AND OSIRIS

foundation of the sacred operations, but some things have moral and needful causes, while others are not without a share in the embellishment of science and physics—as, for instance, in the case of the onion.

2. [The story] that Diktys,[1] the nursling of Isis,[2] fell into the river and was drowned, in trying to catch the onions with his hands,[3] [is] utterly incredible.

3. The priests, however, keep themselves pure of the onion, and treat it hardly, being [ever] on the watch against it, because it is the only thing whose nature is to be well nourished and to flourish when the moon's a-wane.

It's food[4] for neither fast nor feast—neither for the former in that it makes those feeding[5] on it thirst, while for the latter it makes them weep.

4. And in like manner also they consider the sow an unholy animal, because it seems to be covered especially when the moon is on the wane, while the bodies of those who drink its milk burst forth[6] into leprosy[7] and scabrous roughnesses.

5. And the tale (*logos*) they tell after once only[8] sacrificing and eating pig at the full-moon—[namely] that Typhon when pursuing pig towards full-moon found the wooden coffin in which the body of Osiris lay dead, and scattered it in pieces[9]—they do not all receive, thinking it is a trifling mis-hearing [of the true tale] like many more.[10]

6. But they say their ancients so protected themselves against softness [of living] and extravagance and agreeable sensations, that they said a slab was set up in the holy place at Thebes with deprecations in-lettered on it against Meinis[11] the King, who first changed

---

[1] Diktys = the Netter. In other myth-cycles Diktys was son of Poseidon, and is often called simply the Fisher.

[2] *Cf.* xvi, xvii.

[3] ἐπιδρασσόμενον. The Fisher-soul, therefore, presumably fell out of the celestial boat or *baris* of Isis, and the myth may not be quite so ἀπίθανον as Plutarch would have us think. *Cf.* xvii, 3. Ordinary onions do *not* grow in rivers.

[4] Or "fit"—πρόσφορον.

[5] τοὺς προσφερομένους—a word-play on "food".

[6] ἐξανθεῖ—lit., "flower".

[7] λεπρὰν—that which makes the skin scaly and rough (λεπρός, as opposed to λεῖος, smooth); there being also, I believe, a mystical under-meaning in it all.

[8] Apparently once a year.

[9] *Cf.* xviii, 1.

[10] This makes us doubt whether there may not be a number of similar "mis-hearings" in the myth as handed on by Plutarch.

[11] Probably this should be Μνεῦις (Mnevis), the sacred black bull, venerated as the symbol of the *ka* of Rā, and so it may contain some mystical allusion. *Cf.* xxxiii, 5.

the Egyptians from the way of life without riches and without needs and plain.

7. Moreover, Technactis, father of Bocchoris,[1] is said, when marching on the Arabs,[2] when his baggage was delayed,[3] to have used with joy the food nearest at hand, and afterwards to have fallen into deep sleep on a bed of straw,[4] and so embraced frugality; and in consequence of this [he is said] to have execrated the Meinian, and, with the approval of the priests, to have graven his execration on stone.

THE KINGS, THE RIDDLES OF THE PRIESTS, AND THE MEANING OF AMOUN

IX. 1. The kings were appointed from the priests or from the warriors—the one caste possessing worth and honour through manliness, and the other through wisdom.

2. And he who was appointed from the warriors immediately became [one] of the priests and shared in their philosophy—which for the most part was hidden in myths and words (*logoi*), containing dim reflections and transparencies of truth, as, doubtless, they themselves make indirectly plain by fitly setting sphinxes up before the temples, as though their reasoning about the Gods possessed a wisdom wrapped in riddle.[5]

3. Indeed, the seat[6] of Athena (that is Isis, as they think) at Saïs used to have the following inscription on it:

"I am all that has been and is and shall be, and no mortal has ever re-vealed[7] my robe."[8]

4. Moreover, while the majority think that the proper name of

---

[1] τέχνακτις is, perhaps, a word-play on τέχ (√τεκ, τίκτω), "creative" or "generative", and ἀκτίς, "ray"; while βοκχόρις may also be a play—such as, if one is allowed to speculate wildly, βοῦς, "kine", and χορός, "dance", reflecting the celestial βουκόλος or Cowherd.

[2] It is to be noticed that there was an Arab nome in Egypt, and that Egypt was mapped out into a mystic body; and further, that the different surrounding nations were regarded as representative each of certain powers.

[3] Or it may mean "when his filth delayed him", and so contain a mystical implication.

[4] ἐπὶ στιβάδος. It may also mean "on the way".

[5] *Cf.* M. L. *ridellus*, F. *rideau*, a curtain or veil.

[6] The technical term for the sitting statue of a god or goddess.

[7] ἀπεκάλυψεν—that is, no one within duality has expressed or shown that in which this aspect of feminine life veils itself.

[8] For this mystical *logos* of Net (Neith), the Great Mother, *cf.* Budge, *op. cit.*, i, 459 f.

THE MYSTERIES OF ISIS AND OSIRIS

Zeus with the Egyptians is Amoun (which we by a slight change call Ammōn), Manethō, the Sebennyte, considers it His hidden [one], and that His [power of] hiding is made plain by the very articulation of the sound.

5. Hecatæus[1] of Abdēra, however, says that the Egyptians use this word to one another also when they call one to them, for that its sound has got the power of "calling to".[2]

6. Wherefore when they call to the First God—who they think is the same for every man—as unto the Unmanifest and Hidden, invoking Him to make Him manifest and plain to them, they say "Amoun!"

So great, then, was the care Egyptians took about the wisdom which concerned the mysteries of the Gods.

OF THE GREEK DISCIPLES OF EGYPTIANS AND OF PYTHAGORAS AND HIS SYMBOLS

X. 1. And the most wise of the Greeks also are witnesses—Solon, Thales, Plato, Eudoxus, Pythagoras, and, as some say, Lycurgus as well—through coming to Egypt and associating with her priests.

2. And so they say that Eudoxus was hearer of Chonouphis[3] of Memphis, and Solon of Sonchis of Saïs, and Pythagoras of Œnuphis of Heliopolis.

3. And the last especially, as it appears, being contemplated and contemplating,[4] brought back to the memory of his men their[5] symbolic and mysterious [art], containing their dogmas in dark sayings.

4. For most of the Pythagoric messages leave out nothing of what are called the hieroglyphic letters; for instance: "Eat not on what

---

[1] H. flourished 550–475 B.C. A. was a town on the southern shore of Thrace.

[2] προσκλητικήν. H. thus seems to suggest that it (? Amen) was a "word of power", a word of magic for evoking the *ka* of a person, or summoning it to appear. It does not seem very probable that the Egyptians shouted it after one another in the street.

[3] That is, presumably, Knouph or Knef.

[4] θαυμασθείς καὶ θαυμάσας, passive and active of the verb of θαῦμα, generally translated "wonder", but meaning radically "look at with awe"; hence contemplate religiously (the art of θεωρία), and hence the Platonic (? Pythagorean) saying: "The beginning of philosophy is wonder." Compare the variants of the new-found Jesus *logos* ("Let not him who seeks", etc.), which preserve both θαμβηθείς and θαυμάσας.

[5] That is, to the men of Greece the art of the Egyptians.

bears two";[1] "Sit not down on measure";[2] "Plant not phœnix";[3] "Stir not fire with knife[4] in house."

5. And, for myself at least, I think that his men's calling the monad Apollo,[5] and the dyad Artemis, and the hebdomad Athena, and the first cube[6] Poseidon, also resembles those whose statues preside over the sacred places, and whose dramas are acted [there], yea and [the names] painted[7] [there as well].

6. For they write the King and Lord, Osiris,[8] with "eye" and "sceptre".[9] But some interpret the name also as "many-eyed", since in the Egyptian tongue *os* means "many", and *iri* "eye".

7. And they write Heaven, as unageing through eternity,[10] with "heart", [that is] spirit,[11] [rising] from "altar"[12] underneath.

8. And at Thebes there used to be set up hand-less statues of judges, while the [statue] of the chief judge had its eyes tight shut—seeing that Justice neither gives nor takes gift, and is not worked on.

9. And for the warriors, "scarab" was their seal-emblem; for the scarab is not female, but all [scarabs] are male,[13] and they engender their seed into matter [or material] which they make into spheres, preparing a field not so much of nourishment[14] as of genesis.

---

[1] ἐπὶ δίφρου (= δι-φόρου)—variously translated "off a chair", "in a chariot", hence "on a journey". "That which bears two" is that which either carries two or brings forth two; the *logos* is thus, perhaps, a warning against falling into duality of any kind, and hence an injunction to contemplate unity.

[2] The χοῖνιξ was a dry measure, the standard of a man's (slave's) daily allowance of corn. Hence, perhaps, in one sense the symbol may mean: "Be not content with your 'daily bread' only"; yet any meaning connected with "that which measures" would suit the interpretation, such as, "Rest not on measure, but move in the unimmeasurable."

[3] φοῖνιξ means a "Phœnician" (as opposed to an Egyptian), a "date palm" (as opposed to a "pine"), and a "phœnix"; in colour this was "purple red", "purple", or "crimson". The phœnix *proper* rose again from its ashes; *its* colour was golden. φυτύειν means "plant", but also "engender", "beget".

[4] μάχαιρα was, in Homeric times, the technical term for the sacred sacrificial knife—the knife that kills and divides the victim's body, while the fire transmutes and consumes it. There may, perhaps, be some connection between the symbol and the gnomic couplet of Hesiod quoted above (iv, 3); it is, however, generally said to mean, "Do not provoke an angry man", but this leaves out of consideration the concluding words "in house".

[5] *Cf.* lxxv, 14.   [6] Presumably the ogdoad or eight.
[7] Or "written" or "engraved".   [8] Eg. Äsàr.
[9] Generally a "throne" in the hieroglyphs. But for the numerous variants, see Budge, *Gods of the Egyptians*, ii, 113. *Cf.* li, 1, below.
[10] ἀϊδιότητα—lit., form-(or idea-)less-ness; transcending all forms.
[11] θυμόν, one of the most primitive terms of Greek psychology—spirit or soul, or more generally life-principle.
[12] ἐσχάρα, an altar for burnt offerings; here probably symbolising Earth as the syzygy of Heaven.
[13] It is to be remembered that the "mark" of the warriors was their manliness (ix, 1).
[14] Matter (ὕλη) being the Nurse, "according to Plato". The legend was that the scarab beetle deposited its seed into dung which it first made into balls (lxxiv, 5).

THE MYSTERIES OF ISIS AND OSIRIS

ADVICE TO KLEA CONCERNING THE HIDDEN MEANING OF THE MYTHS

XI. 1. When, therefore, thou hearest the myth-sayings of the Egyptians concerning the Gods—wanderings and dismemberings, and many such passions[1]—thou shouldst remember what has been said above, and think none of these things spoken as they [really] are in state and action.

2. For they do not call Hermes "Dog" as a proper name, but they associate the watching and waking from sleep of the animal,[2] who by knowing and not knowing determines friend from foe (as Plato says),[3] with the most Logos-like of the Gods.

3. Nor do they think that the sun rises as a new-born babe from a lotus, but so they *write* "sun-rise", riddling the re-kindling of the sun from moist [elements].[4]

4. Moreover, they called the most crude and awesome King of the Persians (Ōchus)[5]—who killed many and finally cut the throat of Apis and made a hearty meal off him with his friends—"Knife",[6] and they call him so unto this day in the Catalogue[7] of their kings—not, of course, signifying his essence by its proper name,[8] but likening the hardness of his mood[9] to an instrument of slaughter.

5. So too shalt thou, if thou hearest and receivest the [mysteries] about the Gods from those who interpret the myth *purely and according to the love of wisdom*, and if thou doest ever and keepest carefully the customs observed by the priests, and if thou thinkest that thou wilt offer neither sacrifice nor act more pleasing to the Gods than the holding a true view concerning them—thou shalt escape an ill no less than being-without-the-gods,[10] [that is to say] the fearing-of-the-daimones.[11]

---

[1] παθήματα—the technical mystery-term for such experiences, or sensible knowing.

[2] Or "of the Animal"—the Living One or Animal Itself or World Soul, if Dog is taken to mean the genus or Great Dog.

[3] *Rep.*, ii, 375 F.

[4] That is, the ideogram of a new-born child with its finger on its lips seated on the bosom of the lotus signified "sun-rise", and "sun-rise" within as well as without. The "re-kindling" or "lighting up again" was presumably also a symbol of the "new birth from above".

[5] Artaxerxes III; the priests, however, presumably used this incident to illustrate some more general truth. A similar story is also related of Cambyses (xliv, 8); they also called Ōchus "Ass" (xxxi, 4).

[6] The sacrificial knife again, as in x, 2.   [7] *Cf.* xxxviii, 6.

[8] Perhaps even meaning by "his name of power".

[9] Or "of the turn", where it might refer to the turn of Egypt's fate-wheel.

[10] Or "atheism".   [11] Generally rendered "superstition".

XII. 1. The myth which is told is—in its very shortest possible [elements], after the purely useless and superfluous have been removed—as follows:

THE MYSTERY-MYTH

2. They say that when Rhea[1] secretly united with Kronos, Helios on sensing[2] it imprecated her not to bring forth in month or year.[3]

3. That Hermes being in love with the Goddess, came to conjunction [with her]; then playing draughts[4] against Selene,[5] and winning[6] the seventieth of each of the lights, he con-duced from all[7] five days and in-duced them into the three hundred and sixty [days]—which Egyptians call the "now in-duced",[8] and keep as birthdays of the Gods.[9]

4. [And they say] that on the first Osiris was born, and that a voice fell out[10] together with him on his being brought forth—to wit: "The Lord of all forth comes to light."

5. But some say that a certain Pamylē,[11] being moistened[12] from the holy [place] of Zeus, heard a voice directing her to proclaim with outcry that "Great King Good-doing Osiris is born"; and that because of this she nursed Osiris, Kronos entrusting him to her, and they keep with mystic rites the Pamylia in his honour, similar to the Phallephoria.[13]

6. And on the second [they say] Arouēris [was born]—whom they call Apollo, and some call Elder Horus.[14]

---

[1] The Mother of the Gods—"Flowing", that is, motion pure and simple, unordered or chaotic.

[2] In the most primitive meaning of the word αἰσθόμενον—from √αισ lengthened form of αι (compare ἀίω).

[3] μηνὶ μητ' ἐνιαυτῷ. Both words are connected with roots meaning "one" in ancient dialects; μήν=μ-εἰς (Æol.) and ἔνος = an-nus (Lat.). Cf. εἰς, μ-ία, ἔν; hence ἐνι-αυτός = "one-same". The Goddess, therefore, apart from the Sun, could only bring forth in a day.

[4] πέττια,—πεσσός was an oval-shaped stone for playing a game like our draughts; it was also used for the board on which the game was played, divided by five straight lines each way, and therefore into thirty-six squares.

[5] Sc. the moon.   [6] Or "taking away".

[7] Sc. the lights.   [8] ἐπαγομέναις—or "now intercalated".

[9] This is an exceedingly puzzling statement. The "lights" cannot be the "lights" of the moon, of which there were thirty phases. It more probably has some connection with 360, the seventieth of which works out at 5·142857̇—a number not so very far removed from our own calculations. The "each" in the text may thus be an error.

[10] A voice from heaven, a Bath-kol, proceeding from the Womb of Rhea.

[11] παμίλη—presumably a play on πᾶν (all) and ὕλη (matter).

[12] ὑδρευομένην—presumably by the Great Moistener; it is, however, generally translated "drawing water".

[13] That is the "Phallus-Bearing".   [14] Eg. Heru-ur.

THE MYSTERIES OF ISIS AND OSIRIS

On the third that Typhon, neither in season nor in place, but breaking through with a blow, leapt forth through her side.[1]

On the fourth that Isis was born in all moist [conditions].

On the fifth Nephthys, whom they name End and Aphroditē, while some [call] her also Victory.

7. And [they say] that Osiris and Arouēris were from Helios, Isis from Hermes, and Typhon and Nephthys from Kronos, and therefore the kings considering the third[2] of the "induced" [days] nefast, used neither to consult nor serve themselves till night.[3]

8. And [they say] that Nephthys was married to Typhon;[4] but Isis and Osiris being in love with each other, united even before they were born, down in the Womb beneath the Darkness.[5]

9. Some, moreover, say that Arouēris thus came to birth, and that he is called Elder Horus by Egyptians, but Apollo by Greeks.

XIII. 1. And [they say] that when Osiris was king, he straightway set free the Egyptians from a life from which they could find no way out and like unto that of wild beasts,[6] both setting fruits before them, and laying down laws, and teaching them to honour the Gods.

2. And that subsequently he went over the whole earth, clearing it,[7] not in the least requiring arms, but drawing the multitude to himself by charming them with persuasion and reason (*logos*),[8] with song and every art the Muses give;[9] and that for this cause he seems to the Greeks to be the same as Dionysus.[10]

3. And [they say] that while he was away, Typhon attempted no revolution, owing to Isis keeping very careful guard, and having the power[11] in her hands, holding it fast; but that when he [Osiris] came back, he made with art a wile for him, con-juring seventy-two men,

---

[1] πλευρά—meaning in man radically "rib"; also side of a square, and root of a square (or cubic) number. Typhon would be represented by the diagonal.

[2] That is, the birthday of Typhon.

[3] A strange sentence; but as the kings were considered Gods, they probably worshipped themselves, or at least their own *ka*, and consulted themselves as oracles.

[4] Presumably as being opposite, or as hating one another.

[5] *Cf.* liv, 4.

[6] Metaphors reminiscent of the symbolism of the so-called Book of the Dead.

[7] *Sc.* of wild beasts; but may also mean "softening it", when Osiris stands for Water, and again "making it mild", or "civilising it".

[8] He himself being the Logos.

[9] μουσικῆς—music, in the modern meaning of the term, was only one of the arts of the Muses, the nine daughters of Zeus.

[10] Διό-νυσος—that is, "he of the Mount (νῦσα) of Zeus".

[11] That is "sovereignty".

and having as co-worker a queen coming out of Æthiopia, whom they call Asō.[1]

4. But that after measuring out for himself in secret the body of Osiris,[2] and having devised, according to the size,[3] a beautiful and extraordinarily ornamented chest,[4] brought it into the banqueting hall.[5]

5. And that when they were delighted at the sight and wondered, Typhon, in sport, promised to give the chest to him who could make himself exactly equal to it by laying himself down in it.[6]

6. And that when all were trying, one after another, since no one fitted, Osiris stepped in and laid himself down.

7. And they who were present running up, dashed on the lid, and, after some [of them] had closed it down with fastenings, and others had poured hot lead over it, they carried it out to the River,[7] and let it go into the Sea by way of the Tanitic[8] mouth, which [they say] Egyptians call even to this day by a hateful and abominable name.

8. These things they say were done on the seventeenth of the month Athur,[9] in which [month] the Sun passes through the Scorpion; it being the eight-and-twentieth year of Osiris' reign.

---

[1] Probably the prototype of the Alchemical Azoth. Æthiopia was the land of the black folk south of Egypt, the land *par excellence* of the black magicians as opposed to the good ones of the Egyptians (this, of course, being the Egyptian point of view). The Osiris-myth was in Egyptian, presumably, as easily interpretable into the language of magic and con-juration as into other values. Compare the Demotic folk-tales of Khamuas, in Griffith's *Stories of the High Priests of Memphis*, for how this view of it would read in Egyptian. Æthiopia would also mean the Dark Earth as opposed to the Light Heaven.

[2] The "body of Osiris" may mean the cosmos (great or little), as the "body of Adam", its copy in the Kabalah.

[3] Or, "according to the greatness"—using "greatness" in its Gnostic signification, as here meaning the great cosmos and also the cosmic body of man.

[4] In Pythagorean terms, "an odd-ly ordered rectangular encasement"—referring, perhaps, to a certain configuration of cosmic permanent atoms. But see the plate which Isaac Myer calls "A Medieval Idea of the Makrokosm, in the Heavenly Zodiacal Ark", but which intitles itself "*Forma Exterior Arcæ Noē ex Descriptione Mosis*". This is a coffin, and within it lies the dead Christ. The plate is prefixed to p. 439 of Myer's *Qabbalah* (Philadelphia, 1888). It also presumably refers to the "germ" of the cosmic robe of the purified man, the "robe of glory". In mysticism the metaphors cannot be kept unmixed, for it is the apotheosis of syncretism.

[5] Lit., the "drinking together", referring perhaps to the conjunction of certain cosmic forces, and also microcosmically to souls in a state of joy or festivity or bliss, prior to incarnation.

[6] That is, prove the "permanent atoms" were his own—if we think in terms of reincarnation.

[7] *Sc.* the Sacred Nile, Great Jordan, etc., the Stream of Ocean, which, flowing downwards, is the birth of men, and upwards, the birth of Gods.

[8] $\tau\alpha\nu$-$\iota\tau\iota\kappa o\hat{u}$—probably a word-play connected with $\sqrt{\tau\alpha\nu}$, "to stretch", and so make tense or thin, or expand, and so the "wide-stretched mouth of the Great River". *Cf.* the Titans or Stretchers.

[9] Copt. Hathōr—corr. roughly to November.

THE MYSTERIES OF ISIS AND OSIRIS

9. Some, however, say that he had lived and not reigned so long.[1]

XIV. 1. And as the Pans and Satyrs[2] that inhabit round Chemmis[3] were the first to sense the passion[4] [of Osiris], and give tongue concerning what was being done, [they say] that on this account sudden disturbances and emotions of crowds are even unto this day called "panics".

2. But when Isis[5] sensed it, she cut off one of her curls, and put on a mourning dress, whence the city to this day bears the name Koptō.[6]

But others think the name signifies privation,[7] for they say that *koptein* is to de-prive.

3. And [they say] that she, wandering about in every direction, and finding no way out, never approached any one without accosting him; nay, she asked even little children whom she happened to meet, about the chest.

4. And they happened to have seen, and showed the mouth[8] through which the friends of Typhon let the vessel[9] go into the Sea.

5. Because of this [they say] Egyptians believe that little children have prophetic power, and they especially divine from the sounds of their voices, when playing in the holy places and shouting about anything.

6.[10] And [they say] that when [Isis] was aware that Osiris in ignorance had fallen in love and united himself with her sister[11] as with herself, and seeing as proof the honey-clover[12] wreath which he had left behind with Nephthys, she sought for the babe—(for she [N.] exposed it immediately she bore it, through fear of Typhon).[13]

---

[1] *Cf.* xlii, 4.

[2] Two classes of elemental existences.

[3] That is Āpu, the Panopolis of the Greeks; the name Chemmis, the modern Akhmim, is derived from an old Egyptian name. See Budge, *op. cit.*, ii, 188.

[4] πάθος—the technical term of what was enacted in the mystery-drama.

[5] As Mother Nature.

[6] Meaning "I cut"; and in mid. "I cut or beat the breast", as a sign of mourning.

[7] "The depriving things of their power" or "negation"; Osiris being the fertilising or generative or positive power.

[8] *Sc.* the way or passage. In little children the life force is not sexually polarised.

[9] ἀγγεῖον— a vase or vessel of any kind, hence funerary urn or even coffin; but μεταγγίζειν means "to pour from one vessel into another", and μεταγγισμός is the Pythagorean technical term for metempsychosis or palingenesis.

[10] This paragraph, which breaks the narrative, is introduced to give the myth of the birth of Anubis.

[11] *Sc.* Nephthys.

[12] Meli-lote—*lotos* in Greek stands for several plants; it might be translated as "honey-lotus". *Cf.* xxxviii, 5.

[13] Her legitimate spouse.

7. And after it was found with toil and trouble—dogs[1] guiding Isis to it—it was reared and became her guard and follower, being called Anubis, and is said to guard the Gods, as *their* dogs men.

XV. 1. It was from him she got intelligence about the chest:—that after it had been wave-tossed out by the Sea to the Byblos[2] country, the land-wash had gently brought it to rest in a certain "heather-bush."[3]

2. And the heather-bush, in a short time running up into a most beautiful and very large young tree, enfolded, and grew round it,[4] and hid it entirely within itself.

3. And the King,[5] marvelling at the greatness of the tree, after cutting off the branches, and rounding off the trunk that surrounded the coffin without its being seen,[6] set it up as the prop of his roof.

4. And they say that on her hearing of these things by the daimonian spirit of a voice,[7] Isis came to Byblos, and, sitting down at a fountain-head, downcast and weeping, held converse with no one else, but she embraced and showed affection to the maids of the Queen, curling[8] their hair and exhaling from herself on their skin a marvellous fragrance.

5. And when the Queen saw her maids, longing for the ambrosia-smelling hair and skin of the stranger came upon her.

And so when she had been sent for and had become an inmate [of the palace, the Queen] made her nurse of her little one.

6. And the name of the King, they say, was Malkander,[9] while her name according to some was Astarte, according to others Saōsis, and

---

[1] A term used frequently among the Greeks (who presumably got the idea elsewhere) for the servants, agents, or watchers of the higher Gods; thus the Eagle is called the "winged dog" of Zeus (Æsch., *Pr.*, 1022). "Dog", as we have seen (xi, 1, n.), signifies a power of the World, Soul or Great Animal, also of individual souls.

[2] That is, "Papyrus". This Byblos was a "city in the Papyrus Swamps of the Delta". (So Budge, *op. cit.*, ii, 190.)

[3] ἐρείκη—probably a play on the root-meaning of ἐρείκειν, "to quiver", is intended. The Egyptian *erica* was taller and more bushy than ours. Or it may be the tamarisk; elsewhere it is called a mulberry-tree.

[4] Sc. the "coffin"—perhaps here signifying what has lately been called the "permanent atom" in man.

[5] The ruler of the form-side of things.

[6] On the erroneously called "Gnostic" gems, the lopped trunk is a frequent symbol; the lopped "five-branched", presumably.

[7] Notice the three stages of awareness: (i) the babbling of children; (ii) the intelligence given by the dog; (iii) the daimonian spirit of a voice (Heb. *Bath-kol*).

[8] Isis, when she first lost Osiris, cut off a curl (xiv, 2).

[9] Apparently, though curiously, a play on the Semitic *MLK* or *Malek*, "king", and the Greek *andr*, "man"—that is, "king of men".

THE MYSTERIES OF ISIS AND OSIRIS

according to others Nemanous,[1]—or whatever is the name for which the Greek equivalent would be Athenaïs.[2]

XVI. 1. And [they say] that instead of giving it[3] the breast, Isis reared the little one by putting her finger[4] into its mouth, and that at night she burnt round[5] the mortal [elements] of its body, and, turning herself into a swallow, flew round the pillar and twittered a dirge; until the Queen, through spying [on her] and crying out[6] when she saw the babe being burnt round, deprived it of its immortality.[7]

2. That when the Goddess revealed herself, she claimed for herself the pillar of the roof; and, taking it down with the greatest care, she cut away the heather-tree from round it, then wrapping this[8] up in fine linen, and pouring the juices of sweet herbs over it,[9] she placed it in the hands of the royal couple; and even unto this day the people of Byblos venerate the wood[10] lying in the holy place of Isis.

3. As for the coffin, she flung herself round it, and kept moaning so long, that the younger of the little ones of the king died away;[11] and, taking the elder with herself, and placing the coffin on a boat, she sailed away.

4. And when the River Phædrus[12] raised too rough a wind[13] just after dawn,[14] waxing wrath, she dried up his stream.

XVII. 1. And [they say] that when first she found solitude and was

---

[1] Or "Nemanōs". The names seem to have been impartially maltreated by the copyists; thus we find such variants as Aspartē, Sooses, Neimanoë.

[2] There was among the ancients an art of name-translation, as Plato tells us in the Story of Atlantis, in which the Atlantic names, he says, were translated into Greek by Solon or by the priests of Saïs. Here, I believe, there is also a word-play intended. Isis, as we have seen, was pre-eminently Nurse, τίτθη, a further intensification of the intensified τι-θη from √θα, "suckle"; the common form of "nurse" was τι-θή-νη. On the contrary, ἀθηναίς is a daughter or derivative of ἀ-θή-νη, one who does not give suck; for Athena was born from the head and was the virgin goddess *par excellence*. Mythologically, Athenaïs was wife of Alalkomeneus, the eponymous hero of a city in Bœotia, where was a very ancient temple of Athena. In the Pindaric ode quoted in S. (1) of chapter, "Myth of Man in the Mysteries", Alalkomeneus is given as one of the equivalents for the "first man".

[3] The child's name was Diktys, according to viii, 2.

[4] The √δεκ in δάκτυλος is said to be the same as that in δέκα, "ten", and "ten" is the number of "perfection".

[5] Or "away".

[6] Lit., "croaking" like a raven, to match the "twittering" of the swallow.

[7] This presumably hints that Isis, as the Divine Mother, endeavours to make all perfect and sound, while the earthly mother prevents this.

[8] Sc. the *erica*.

[9] Cf. John xix, 40: "So they took the body of Jesus and wrapped it in fine linen together with sweet herbs."

[10] τὸ ξύλον—the term used repeatedly in the New Testament for the cross.

[11] Or "swooned", or lost consciousness.

[12] φαίδρος—lit., Bright, Beaming, Shining—that is, the Sun-stream.

[13] Or "breath" (πνεῦμα). [14] That is "at sun-rise".

by herself, she opened the chest, and laying her face on his face, she kissed [him] and shed tears.

2. And that when the little one came up in silence from behind and understood, on sensing it she turned herself about, and passionately gave him an awe-ful look. And the little one could not hold himself up against the awe of her, and died.

3. But some say [it was] not thus, but, as it has been said before,[1] that he fell out[2] into the river.

4. And he has honours owing to the Goddess, for the Maneros[3] whom Egyptians hymn at their symposia is he.

5. While others relate that the boy was called Palæstinos[4] or Pelousios, and that the city[5] was named after him when it was founded by the Goddess; and that the Maneros who is hymned was the first to discover the art of the Muses.[6]

6. But some say that it is the name of no one, but a manner of speech for men drinking and feasting—with the meaning "May such and such things be present in becoming measure!" For the Egyptians on every such occasion shout out this, it being indicated to them by "Maneros".

7. Just as, doubtless, also their being shown the image of a dead man carried round in a small wooden coffin, is not a reminder of the Osirian passion, as some suppose; but it is in order to exhort them while filled with wine to make use of things present, in that all will very presently be such [as it], that they bring in an unpleasing after-revel.

XVIII. 1. And [they say] that when Isis had gone a journey to her son Horus, who was being reared at Boutos,[7] and had put away[8] the chest,[9] Typhon, taking his dogs[10] out by night towards the moon, came upon it; and recognising the body, tore it into fourteen pieces, and scattered them abroad.

---

[1] *Cf.* viii, 2.   [2] *Sc.* of the boat of Isis.

[3] Μαν-έρως. I fancy this is a play, in conjunction with the κατα-μαν-θάν-οντα and ἀπο-θάν-οντα (the "understanding" and "dying away") above; the name would then mean either "love of understanding" or "understanding of love".

[4] παλαιστινός—perhaps a play on παλαιστής, "a wrestler"; hence a "rival" or "suitor".

[5] Pelusium; the Pelusian was the eastern mouth of the Nile.

[6] See note on xxi, 1.

[7] Generally supposed to stand for the city Butō, but may be some word-play. Can it be connected with Boötes, the Ploughman—the constellation Arcturus—the voyage being celestial; that is, a movement of the world-soul or change of state in the individual soul? Budge (p. 192) gives its Egyptian equivalent as Per-Uatchit, *i.e.* "House of the Eye".

[8] Lit., from her feet.   [9] Lit., vessel; may also mean "cell".   [10] *Vulg.*, "hunting".

THE MYSTERIES OF ISIS AND OSIRIS

2. And Isis [they say] on learning this, searched for them in a papyrus skiff (*baris*) sailing away through the marshes;[1] whence those who sail in papyrus hulls are not injured by the crocodiles, either because they[2] fear or rather revere the Goddess.[3]

3. And it is because of this [they say] that many tombs of Osiris are spoken of in Egypt[4]—through her performing burial rites on meeting with each piece.

4. Some, however, say no; but that making herself images [of them] she distributed these to each city,[5] as though she were giving it the [whole] body, in order that it might have honours from the multitude, and that even if Typhon should get the better of Horus, he might renounce his search for the true tomb when many were spoken of and pointed out.

5. Now, the only one of the parts of Osiris which Isis did not find was that which causes awe; for that it was cast straightway into the River, and the scaly-coat,[6] and the devourer,[7] and the sharp-snout[8] ate it up—which [they say] among fishes are considered specially expiate;[9] and that Isis, making herself a counterfeit instead of it, consecrated the phallus; in honour of which the Egyptians keep festival even to this day.[10]

XIX. 1. Thereafter Osiris, coming to Horus out of the Invisible,[11] worked through him and trained him for the fight.

2. He then put this test question to him: "What does he consider fairest?" And when he said: "Helping father and mother in ill plight"—he asked a second: "What animal does he think most useful for those who go out to fight?"

---

[1] ἕλη—a probable play on the δι-ελεῖν ("tear to pieces") above.
[2] *Sc.* the crocodiles.
[3] It is remarkable how that every now and then Plutarch inserts apparently the most naïve superstitions without a word of explanation. They cannot be all simply irresponsible *on dits*. It is, perhaps, not without significance that the "chest" is first of all drifted to the Papyrus country, and that the *baris* of Isis should be made of papyrus. It seems almost as if it symbolised some "vehicle" that was safe from the "crocodile" of the deep. In other words, the skiffs are not paper boats and the crocodiles not alligators.
[4] "And Egypt *they say* is the body"—to quote a refrain from Hippolytus concerning the "Gnostics".
[5] Presumably of the fourteen sacred ones.
[6] λεπιδωτόν. [7] φάγρον. [8] ὀξύρυγχον.
[9] Anthropologically, "taboo".
[10] What these "fourteen parts" of Osiris may be is beyond the sphere of dogmatism. I would suggest that there may be along one line some connection with those seeds of life which have lately been called "permanent atoms"; and along another line, that of the birth of the Christ-consciousness, there may be a series of powers derived from past incarnations.
[11] Hades.

3. And when Horus said "Horse", he marvelled at him, and was quite puzzled why he did not say "Lion" rather than "Horse".[1]

4. Accordingly Horus said: "'Lion' is a needful thing to one requiring help, but 'Horse' [can] scatter in pieces the foe in flight and consume him utterly."[2]

Thus hearing, Osiris rejoiced that Horus was fitly prepared.

5. And it is said that as many were changing over to the side of Horus, Thūēris,[3] Typhon's concubine, came, too; and that a certain serpent pursuing after her was cut in pieces by those round Horus.[4] And today on this account they cast down a small rope and cut it in pieces for all to see.[5]

6. The fight lasted for many days, and Horus won. Nevertheless, when Isis received Typhon in bonds, she did not make away with him. Far from it; she unbound him and let him go.

7. Horus, however, did not bear this temperately; but, laying hands on his mother, he drew off the crown from her head. Whereupon Hermes[6] crowned her with a head-dress of cow-horns.

8. And [they say] that also when Typhon got the chance of bringing a bastardy suit against Horus, and Hermes was counsel for the defence, Horus was judged legitimate by the Gods.[7]

And that [afterwards] Typhon was fought under in two other fights.

9. And that Isis brought forth from her union with Osiris after his death[8] Harpocrates[9]—who missed the month and was weak in his limbs from below upwards.[10]

THE UNDER-MEANING, A REFLEXION OF A CERTAIN REASON

XX. 1. These are approximately the chief headings of their myth, after the most ill-omened have been removed—such as, for instance,

---

[1] The "Horse" may symbolise purified passion, and "Lion" a certain receptive power of the mind.
[2] The white "Horse" was presumably opposed to the red "Ass" of Typhon, as the purified vehicle of the soul contrasted with the impure. "Lion" was one of the grades in the Mithriac Mysteries; it was a sun-animal.
[3] Eg. Ta-urt (Budge, *op. cit.*, p. 193).
[4] That is, by the Companions of Horus (or Disciples of the Christ)—a frequent scene in the vignettes of the Book of the Dead.
[5] That is, in the public mystery processions.
[6] The symboliser as well as the interpreter of the Gods.
[7] Cf. liv, 3.
[8] Or it may mean "completion" ($\tau\epsilon\lambda\epsilon\upsilon\tau\acute{\eta}\nu$).
[9] In Eg. Ḥeru-p-khart, *i.e.* "Horus the Younger".
[10] τοῖς κάτωθεν γυίοις—but, presumably, not from above downwards.

THE MYSTERIES OF ISIS AND OSIRIS

the one about the cutting up into pieces of Horus, and the beheading of Isis.

2. That, however, if people suppose and say these things about that Blessed and Incorruptible Nature according to which especially the Divine conceives itself, as though they were actually enacted and really took place, "thou shouldst spit out and cleanse mouth", according to Æschylus,[1] there is no need to tell thee;[2] for of thyself thou showest displeasure at those who hold illegitimate and barbarous notions about the Gods.

3. But that these things are not at all like lean tales and quite empty figments, such as poets and prose-writers weave and expand as though they were spiders spinning them out of themselves from a source that has no basis in fact, but that they contain certain informations and statements—thou knowest of thyself.

4. And just as the Mathematici[3] say that "Iris"[4] is the sun's reflexion many-coloured by the return of its visual impression to the cloud, so the myth down here is a reflexion of a certain reason (*logos*) that bends its thinking back on other things; as both the sacred offerings suggest by the reflected element of mournfulness and sadness they contain, and also the dispositions of the temples which in one direction open out into side-walks and courts for moving about in, open to the sky and clear of objects, while in the other they have hidden and dark robing-rooms under ground, like places for putting coffins in and burying-spots.

CONCERNING THE TOMBS OF OSIRIS

5. And not least of all does the belief of the Osirians—since the body [of Osiris] is said to be in many places—[suggest this].

6. For they say that both Diochitē is called Polichnē,[5] because it alone has the true one; and [also] that it is at Abydos that the wealthy and powerful of the Egyptians are mostly buried—their ambition being to have a common place of burial with the body of Osiris; and [again] that it is at Memphis that the Apis is reared as the image of the soul of Osiris, because it is *there* also that his body lies.

---

[1] Ed. Nauck, p. 84.
[2] *Sc.* Klea.
[3] Presumably, again, the Pythagorean grade above the Hearers.
[4] *Sc.* the rainbow.
[5] Either the reading is at fault, or some word-play is intended. Dio-chitē is probably Zeus-something; but I cannot resolve it. While Polichnē is a rare diminutive of πόλις, and would thus mean "Little City".

7. And as for the City,[1] some interpret it as "Harbour of Good Things", but others give it the special meaning of "Tomb of Osiris"; it is, however, the little island one[2] at Philæ [they say] which is in other respects inaccessible and inapproachable by all, and that not even the birds light on it or fish come near it, but at a certain season the priests cross over [to it] and make offerings to the dead, and place wreaths on the monument which is overshadowed by a . . .[3] tree, which is greater in size than any olive.

XXI. 1. Eudoxus, however, [says] that, though many tombs are spoken of in Egypt, the body lies at Būsiris, for that this had been the native city of Osiris; nevertheless Taphosiris requires no further reason [to establish its claim], for the name explains itself—namely, "Burying of Osiris".

"But I rede of cutting of wood, of rending of linen, and pouring of pourings, because many of the mystery-[meanings] have been mixed up with them."[4]

[1] ? Memphis; or, perhaps, as contrasted with the Little City above.

[2] *Sc.* city; νισιτάνην is a hopeless reading, and as the editors can make nothing out of it, I suggest νησίτιδα or νησιδάνην (πόλιν).

[3] μηθίδης—apparently an error; Bernardakis suggests μίνθης (Lat. *mentha*), "mint". Can the right reading be μηδικῆς (πόας)? The *herba medica* was, however, the sainfoin or lucerne, which, though reminding us of the melilote of xiv, is hardly capable of overshadowing a tomb even in the most intricate symbolical sense.

[4] Evidently a verbal quotation from Eudoxus. The "cutting of wood" presumably refers to the trunk with lopped branches, which, as we have already mentioned, occurs so frequently on so-called "Gnostic" gems; the "rending of linen" (λίνου) might also be made to refer to Linus, the Bard, and his being torn to pieces like Osiris; *Linos* also means the "Song of Linus", so called, it is supposed by some, because in earliest times the strings of the cithara were made of flax. For other names of singers used for lays or modes of song, compare Manerōs and Pæan; though, of course, the modern way is to regard the singer as the personification of the lay. Thus in Emil Naumann's *History of Music* (trans. by F. Praeger; London, 1882), p. 3, we read: "The Greek tribes of Peloponnesus and Hellas, as well as the Egyptians, Phœnicians, the Greeks inhabiting the isles of the Ægean Sea, and especially those of Cyprus, had a primitive 'Lament' which seems to have come originally from Phœnicia. It was a funeral chant on the death of the youthful Adonis. . . . The Egyptians changed its signification into a lament of Isis for Osiris. The Greeks called it *Linos*, and the Egyptians *Maneros*." The beginning of the "Manerōs", or the Lament of Isis for her Beloved, is given as follows by Naumann (p. 40):

"Return, oh return!
God Panu, return!
Those that were enemies are no more here.
Oh lovely helper, return,
That thou may'st see me, thy sister,
Who loves thee.
And com'st thou not near me?
O beautiful youth, return, oh, return!
When I see thee not
My heart sorrows for thee,
My eyes ever seek thee,
I roam about for thee, to see thee in the form of the Nai,

THE MYSTERIES OF ISIS AND OSIRIS

2. But the priests say that not only of these Gods, but also of all the other gods also who are not ingenerable and indestructible, the bodies lie buried with them when they[1] have done their work, and have service rendered them, while their souls shine in heaven as stars; and that [of the former] the [soul] of Isis is called Dog by the Greeks, but Sōthis by the Egyptians, while the [soul] of Horus [is called] Ōriōn,[2] and Typhon's Bear.[3]

3. And [they say] that for the burials of the animals to whom honour is paid, the rest [of the Egyptians] pay the [dues which are] mutually determined; but that those alone who inhabit the Thebaid give nothing, since they believe that no God is subject to death, and that he whom they themselves call Knēph is ingenerable and immortal.

CONCERNING THE THEORY OF EVEMERUS

XXII. 1. Now, since many of such [? tombs] are spoken of and pointed out, those who think these [myths] commemorate the awe-inspiring and mighty works and passions of kings and tyrants who, through surpassing virtue and power, put in a claim for the reputation of divinity, and afterwards experienced reverses of fortune—employ a very easy means of escape from the [true] reason (*logos*), and not unworthily transfer the ill-omened [element in them] from Gods to men, and they have the following to help them from the narratives related.

2. For instance, the Egyptians tell us that Hermes had a short-armed[4] body, that Typhon was red-skinned, Horus white, and Osiris black, as though they were [men] born in the course of nature.

To see thee, to see thee, thou beautiful lov'd one.
Let me the Radiant, see thee
God Panu, All-Glory, see thee again!
To thy belovèd come, blessed Onnòfris,
Come to thy sister, come to thy wife,
God Urtuhet, oh, come!
Come to thy consort!"

Unfortunately, Naumann does not give any references by which we can control his statements.

[1] The bodies; presumably referring to the mummies of those men and women who were believed to have reached the god-stage while living.

[2] *Cf.* xxii, 3.

[3] Probably all name-plays: κύων (dog), √κυ (conceive)—see lxi, 6; H-ōr-os, Ōr-iōn; ἄρκ-τος (bear), √αρκ (suffice, endure, bear); Ursa Major is called the Wain.

[4] γαλι-άγκωνα—lit., weasel-armed. Now, as we are told further on (lxxiv, 3) that the weasel (γαλῆ), or marten, was fabled to conceive through the ear and bring forth through the mouth, this animal was evidently a symbol of mind-conception. "Weasel-armed" may thus symbolise some faculty of the interpretative mind (Hermes).

3. Moreover, also, they call Osiris "General" and Kanōbus[1] "Pilot"—from whom, they say, the star got its name.

And [they say] that the ship which Greeks call Argō is an image of the bark of Osiris, constellated in his honour, and that it sails not far from Ōriōn and Dog, the former of which Egyptians consider the sacred [boat] of Horus and the latter of Isis.[2]

XXIII. 1. But I am afraid that this is "moving the immoveable", and "warring" not only "against many centuries", according to Simōnidēs,[3] but "against many nations of men" and races held fast by religious feeling towards these Gods—when people let nothing alone but transfer such mighty names from heaven to earth, and [so] banish and dissolve the sense of worship and faith that has been implanted in nearly all [men] from their first coming into existence, opening up wide entrances for the godless folk,[4] and reducing the divine [mysteries] to the level of men's doings, and giving a splendid licence to the charlatanries of Evemerus[5] the Messenian, who of himself composing the counterpleas of a baseless science of myths unworthy of any credit, flooded the civilised world with sheer atheism, listing off level all those who are looked on as gods into names of generals and admirals and kings, who (he is good enough to say) existed in bygone days, and are recorded in letters of gold at Panchōn[6]—which [records] neither any non-Greek nor any Greek has ever come across, but Evemerus alone, when he went his voyage to the Panchoans and Triphyllians, who never have been nor are anywhere on earth.

XXIV. 1. And yet mighty deeds of Semiramis are sung of among Assyrians, and mighty [deeds] of Sesōstris in Egypt. And Phrygians even unto this day call splendid and marvellous doings "manic", owing to the fact that Manes, one of their bygone kings, proved himself a good and strong man among them—the one whom some call Mazdes.[7] Cyrus led Persians and Alexander Macedonians, con-

---

[1] Canopus was fabled to be the pilot of the bark of Osiris; in Greek mythology he was the pilot of the General Menelaos on his return from Troy.

[2] Cf. xxi, 2.

[3] Bergk, iii, 522.

[4] Or "atheists". "An evident allusion to the Christians", says King (in loc.); but we think Plutarch was more impersonal than his commentator.

[5] E. flourished in the last quarter of the fourth century B.C.

[6] The capital, presumably, of the mythical island of Panchæa, which was supposed to be somewhere on the southern coast of Asia, and to which Evemerus pretended he had sailed on a voyage down the Red Sea.

[7] King notes: "The common title of the Sassanean kings was 'Masdesin'—'servant of Ormazd'."

THE MYSTERIES OF ISIS AND OSIRIS

quering to almost the ends of the earth; still they have the name and memory of good kings [only].

2. "And if some elated by vast boastfulness," as Plato says,[1] "concomitant with youth and ignorance, through having their souls inflamed with pride," have accepted titles like gods and dedications of temples, their glory has flourished for a short time [only], and afterwards they have incurred the penalty of vanity and imposture coupled with impiety and indecency:[2]

Death coming swift on them, like smoke they rose and fell.[3]

And now like runaway [slaves] that can be lawfully taken, torn from the temples and altars, they have naught but their tombs and graves.

3. Wherefore Antigonus the Elder, when a certain Hermodotus, in his poems, proclaimed him "Son of the Sun and God", remarked: "My night-stool boy has not so exalted an opinion of me."

And with reason also did Lysippus, the sculptor, blame Apelles, the painter, for putting a thunderbolt in Alexander's hand when painting his portrait; whereas he himself gave him a spear-head—from which not even time itself shall take away the glory, for it is true and really his.

THE THEORY OF THE DAIMONES

XXV.[4] 1. They, therefore, [do] better who believe that the things related about Typhon and Osiris and Isis are passions neither of gods nor of men, but of mighty daimones, who—as Plato and Pythagoras and Xenocrates and Chrysippus say, following the theologers of bygone days—have been born more manful than men, far surpassing us in the strength of their nature, yet not having the divine unmixed and pure, but proportioned with the nature of soul and sense of body, susceptible of pleasure and pain and all the passions, which as innate to such metamorphoses trouble some [of them] more and others less.

2. For the Gigantic and Titanic [Passions] sung of among the Greeks, and certain lawless deeds of Kronos and antagonisms of Pythōn against Apollo, and fleeings of Dionysus, and wanderings of Demeter, in no way fall behind the Osiric and Typhonic [Passions], and others which all may hear unrestrainedly spoken of in myth.

---
[1] *Legg.*, 716 A.
[2] A bold thing to write in an age of Emperor-divinising.
[3] Apparently from an otherwise unknown poet. See Bergk, iii, 637.
[4] This chapter is quoted by Eusebius, *Præp. Ev.*, V, v, 1.

And all these things which, under the veil of mystic sacred rites and perfectionings, are carefully kept from being spoken of to, or being allowed to be seen by, the multitude, have a similar reason (*logos*).[1]

XXVI. 1. Moreover, we hear Homer also on every occasion calling the good variously "godlike" and "equal to gods", and as "having directions[2] from gods"; whereas he employs epithets connected with the daimones to both worthy and unworthy in common:

Draw nigh, thou daimonian! Why so fearest the Argives?[3]

And again:

But when indeed for the fourth time he charged, a daimon's equal.[4]

And: O thou daimonian! what so great ills do Priam now
And Priam's sons to thee, that thou dost hotly rage
Troy's well-built town to rase?[5]

—as though the daimones possessed a mixed and an unbalanced nature and propensity.

2. For which reason Plato[6] refers unto the God upon Olympus' height things "right" and "odd",[7] and to the daimones those that respond to these.[8]

3. Moreover, Xenocrates[9] thinks that the nefast days, and all the holy days on which are strikings or beatings or fastings or blasphemies or foul language, have nothing to do with honours paid to gods or to beneficent daimones; but that there are natures in the circumambient,[10] mighty and powerful indeed, but difficult to turn and sullen, who take pleasure in such things, and when they get them turn to nothing worse.

4. The beneficent and good ones, again, Hesiod also calls "holy daimones" and "guardians of men"—"wealth-givers and possessors of this sovereign prerogative".[11]

5. Plato[12] again gives to this race the name of hermeneutic and of diaconic[13] 'twixt Gods and men, speeding up thitherwards men's vows and prayers, and bringing thence prophetic answers hitherwards and gifts of [all] good things.

---

[1] *Sc.* to the mysteries of the Egyptians. [2] μήδεα—also meaning *virilia*.
[3] *Il.*, xiii, 810. [4] *Il.*, v, 438. [5] *Il.*, iv, 31 f. [6] *Legg.*, 717 A.
[7] Pythagorean technical terms.
[8] τὰ ἀντίφωνα—the meaning seeming to be rather that of "concord" than of "discord".
[9] An immediate pupil of Plato's.
[10] The air or ether that surrounds the earth.
[11] *Op. et Dies*, 126. [12] *Symp.*, 202 E. [13] That is, "interpretative and ministering".

THE MYSTERIES OF ISIS AND OSIRIS

6. Whereas Empedocles[1] says that the daimones have to amend whatever faults they make, or discords they may strike:

"For æther's rush doth chase them seawards; sea spews them on land's flat; and earth into the beams of tireless sun; and he casts [them again] into the swirls of æther. One takes them from another, and all abhor [them]"[2]—until after being thus chastened and purified they regain their natural place and rank.

XXVII. 1. Born from the self-same womb as these and things like them, they say, are the legends about Typhon: how that he wrought dire deeds through envy and ill-will, and after throwing all things into confusion and filling the whole earth and sea as well with ills, he afterwards did make amends.

2. But the sister-wife[3] of Osiris who upheld his honour, after she had quenched and laid to rest Typhon's frenzy and fury, did not allow forgetfulness and silence to overtake the struggles and trials he had endured, and her own wanderings and many [deeds] of wisdom, and many [feats] of manliness; but intermingling with the most chaste perfectionings images and under-meanings and copies of the passion she then endured, she hallowed at one and the same time a lesson of religion and a consolation to men and women placed in like circumstances.

3. And she and Osiris, being changed through virtue from good daimones into gods[4]—as [were] subsequently Heracles and Dionysus—possess the dignities of gods and daimones at one and the same time, fitly combined everywhere indeed but with the greatest power among those above earth and under earth.

CONCERNING SARAPIS

4. For they say that Sarapis is no other than Pluto, and Isis Persephassa, as Archemachus of Eubœa has said,[5] and Heracleides of Pontus, when he supposes that the seat of the oracle at Canopus is Pluto's.

---

[1] E. flourished 494–434 B.C.

[2] Stein, 377 ff.; Karsten, 16 ff.; Fairbanks, p. 204. The quotation appears to me inapposite, for Empedocles seems to be speaking of "any who defile their bodies sinfully" and not of daimones; but perhaps the "received" recombination of the fragments is at fault.

[3] See the note on "sister-wife" in comment on Mariamnē (Hipp., *Philos.*—Introd.) in chapter on "Myth of Man".—Prolegg., p. 102, n. 2.

[4] That *is* to say, according to this theory the myth represented the degree of initiation by which a man passed from the stage of daimon into the state of god, or from super-man to Christ.

[5] Müller, iv, 315.

XXVIII. 1. And Ptolemy the Saviour[1] saw in a dream the gigantic statue of Pluto—though he had not previously seen or known what form it was—ordering him to bring it to Alexandria.

2. And when he did not know and had no idea where [the statue] was set up even after he had described his vision to his friends, there was found a man, a great traveller, by name Sōsibius, who said he had seen at Sinopē just such a colossus as the King seemed to have seen.

3. He [Ptolemy] accordingly sent Sōtelēs and Dionysius, who, after expending much time and pains, not, however, without the help of God's providence, removed it secretly and brought it away.

4. And when it had been brought [to Alexandria] and set up publicly, the assistants of Timotheus, the interpreter, and of Manethōs, the Sebennyte, coming to the conclusion that it was a statue of Pluto—judging by its cerberus and huge serpent—convinced Ptolemy that it was that of no other of the Gods than Sarapis; for it did not come from Sinopē with this designation, but after it had been brought to Alexandria it received the Egyptian name for Pluto, namely, Sarapis.

5. And yet people sink into the opinion of Heracleitus the physicist, when he says: "Hades[2] and Dionysus are the same, for whomsoever they rage and riot."

For those who postulate that Hades means the body, because the soul is as it were deranged and drunken in it, put forward a [too] meagre interpretation.

6. But [it is] better to identify Osiris with Dionysus, and Sarapis[3] with Osiris, so designated after he had changed his nature.[4] Wherefore "Sarapis" is common to all,[5] just as, you know, those who share in the sacred rites know that "Osiris" is.

XXIX. 1. For it is not worth while paying attention to the Phrygian writings, in which Isis is said to have been the daughter of Charops,[6] son of Heracles, and Typhon [son] of Æacus,[7] [also] son of Heracles.

2. Nor [is it worth while] refraining from disregarding Phylarchus,[8] when he writes that "it was Dionysus who first brought two

---

[1] The first Greek King of Egypt, 324–285 B.C.
[2] That is, Pluto.
[3] Sar-apis—a combination of Osiris and Apis, the soul of Osiris; cf. xxix, 5. In Eg. Asār-Hāpi.
[4] Presumably from that of a daimon to that of a god.
[5] That is, apparently, a common principle in all men.
[6] Lit. "Bright-(or Glad-)eyed".
[7] Lit., "Wailer".   [8] A historian; flourished c. 215 B.C.

THE MYSTERIES OF ISIS AND OSIRIS

oxen from India to Egypt, of which the name of one was Apis, and of the other Osiris; and *Sarapis* is the name of Him who orders [or adorns] the universe from *sairein* ['sweep', 'clean'], which some say [means] 'beautifying' and 'adorning' ";—for these [remarks] of Phylarchus are absurd.

3. But still more so are those of them who say that Sarapis is not a god, but that the coffin of Apis[1] is thus named, and that certain brazen gates at Memphis, called "Gates of Oblivion and Wailing", open with a deep mournful sound, when they bury Apis, and that therefore at every sounding of brass[2] we are plunged into oblivion.

4. More moderate are they who claim that the simultaneous motion of the universe is thus called [*sc. Sarapis*], from *seuesthai* and *sousthai*[3] ["speed"].

5. But the majority of the priests say that "Osiris" and "Apis" have been woven together into the same [name], explaining and teaching that we should look on the Apis as an en-formed image of the soul of Osiris.

6. If, however, the name of Sarapis is Egyptian, I for my part think it denotes "Good Cheer" and "Delight"—finding a proof in the fact that Egyptians call the feast "Delights"—*Sairei*.

And, indeed, Plato says that Hades has been so called as being "sweet"[4] and gentle to those with him.

7. And with Egyptians both many other of their names are *logoi*,[5] and they call subterrene space, to which they think the souls depart after death, Amenthē—the name signifying "the [space] which takes and gives".[6]

8. But whether this, too, is one of the names that left Hellas long

---

[1] "Ἄπιδος σόρον—another word-play, "*sor-apis*".

[2] ἠχοῦντος ... χαλκώματος. This has, nevertheless, presumably some mystic meaning. In the myths, cymbals were said to have been used to protect the infant Bacchus, and infant Zeus, and to keep off the Titans—so, presumably, plunging them into oblivion. Compare also I Corinth. xiii, 1, where Paul, speaking of the exercise of the "gift of tongues" (*glossalaly*) without love (ἀγάπη), uses precisely the same term, when saying: "I am become as sounding brass (χαλκὸς ἠχῶν) or tinkling cymbal"—the latter being, perhaps, a reference to the *sistrum*, while the former is perhaps a metaphor, derived from the hardness and colour ("red") of brass, or rather bronze or copper, referring to a state of mind which plunges us into oblivion of our better part—namely, spiritual love.

[3] A contracted form of the former—from √σϜε or √σεϜ, with idea of "swiftness". (?) Serapis—sev-a-this—sevesthai.

[4] ἀδούσιον—unknown to the lexicons. I suggest that it may be connected with ἡδος, from √σϜαδ of ἀνδάνω—hence "sweet".

[5] Presumably "words of deep meaning"—another technical use of this Proteus-like term.

[6] Budge (*op. cit.*, ii, 200) says: "The Egyptian form of the word is Amentet, and the name means 'hidden place'."

ago and have been brought back again,[1] we will examine later on; for the present, let us continue with the remaining [points] of the belief we have in hand.

CONCERNING TYPHON

XXX. 1. Osiris and Isis have, then, changed from good daimones into gods. While as for the dimmed and shattered power of Typhon, though it is at the last gasp and in its final death-throes, they still appease and soothe it with certain feasts of offerings.

2. Yet, again, every now and then at certain festivals they humiliate it dreadfully and treat it most despitefully—even to rolling red-skinned men in the mud, and driving an ass over a precipice (as the Koptos folk), because Typhon was born with his skin red and ass-like. While the Busiris folk and Lycopolitans do not use trumpets at all, as they sound like an ass [braying].

3. And generally they think that the ass is not clean, but a daimonic animal, on account of its resemblance to that [god]; and making round-cakes for feasts of offerings on both the month of Paÿni and that of Phaōphi,[2] they stamp on them an "ass tied".[3]

4. And on the Feast of Offerings of the Sun, they pass the word to the worshippers not to wear on the body things made of gold nor to give food to an ass.[4]

5. The Pythagorics also seem to consider Typhon a daimonic power; for they say that Typhon was produced on the six-and-fiftieth even measure; and again that the [power][5] of the equilateral triangle is that of Hades and Dionysus and Ares; that of the square is that of Rhea and Aphrodite and Demeter and Hestia (that is, Hera); that of the dodecagon, that of Zeus; and that of the fifty-six angled [regular polygon], that of Typhon—as Eudoxus relates.[6]

XXXI. 1. And, as Egyptians believe that Typhon was born red-

[1] How very Greek! Cf. lxi, 4.
[2] Copt. Paōni and Paopi—corr. roughly with June and October.
[3] ὄνον δεδεμένον. Cf. Matt. xxi, 2: ὄνον δεδεμένην; cf. also l, 3, where it is a hippopotamus.
[4] That is, presumably, not to weigh down their minds with the superfluity of riches, nor to feed up the stupid and lustful energies of their souls.
[5] A "power" in Pythagorean technology is the side of a square (or, perhaps, of any equilateral polygon) in geometry; and in arithmetic the square root, or that which being multiplied into itself produces the square.
[6] Eudoxus seems to have been Plutarch's authority for his statements regarding Pythagorean doctrine; cf. vi, lii, lxii. The Typhonic figure might be generated by "sevening" the interior angles of a regular octagon and producing the radii to the circumference of the circumscribed circle, or by "eighting" the interior angles of a regular heptagon.

THE MYSTERIES OF ISIS AND OSIRIS

skinned,[1] they offer in sacrifice even the red ones of the oxen [only] after making the scrutiny so close, that if [the beast] has even a single hair black or white, they consider it ought not to be offered; for if it were sacrificed, it would not be an acceptable offering to the gods, but the contrary, [as are] all those animals which have seized on the souls of impure and unrighteous men in the course of their transformation into bodies other [than human].

2. Wherefore after uttering imprecations on the head of the victim,[2] and cutting off its head, they used to cast it into the river in olden days, but nowadays they give it to strangers.

3. But as to the one that is to be sacrificed, those of the priests who are called Sealers, set a mark upon it—the seal (as Kastōr[3] relates) having the impression of a man forced down on one knee with his hands drawn round behind him, and a sword sticking in his throat.[4]

4. And they think that the ass also has the distinction of its resemblance [to Typhon], as has been said, owing to its aversion to being taught and to its wantonness, no less than on account of its skin.[5]

5. For which cause also since they especially detested Ōchus[6] of [all] the Persian kings as being blood-polluted and abominable, they gave him the nickname of "Ass".

But he, with the retort: "This Ass, however, will make a fine feast off your Ox"—slaughtered the Apis, as Deinōn has told us.[7]

6. Those, however, who say that Typhon's flight from the fight on an ass lasted seven days, and that after reaching a place of safety he begat sons—Hierosolymus and Judæus—are instantly convicted of dragging Judaïc matters into the myth.[8]

THE THEORY OF THE PHYSICISTS

XXXII. 1.[9] The above [data] then afford [us] such and such suggestions. But from another start let us consider the simplest of those who seem to give a more philosophical explanation.

---

[1] Or "fire-coloured".

[2] Compare the Ritual of Azāzel (the scape-goat), one of the two goats set apart on the Great Day of Atonement among the Jews (Lev. xvi, 8 ff.).

[3] *Cf.* also Plut., *Ætia Romana*, x. Castor was a Greek historian who was a contemporary of Cicero and Julius Cæsar.

[4] The ox was, therefore, the vicarious atonement of the man.

[5] It was a red ass, then, which symbolised the Typhonic power.   [6] *Cf.* xi, 4.

[7] Müller, ii, 95. Deinōn was a contemporary of Alexander the Great, and wrote a history of Persia.

[8] This item of ancient scandal would almost seem to have come from the pen of an Apion; it is an interesting specimen of theological controversy in story-form.

[9] This paragraph and the next is quoted by Eusebius, *Præp. Ev.*, III, iii, 11.

2. These are those who say that, just as the Greeks allegorise time as Kronos, and air as Hera, and the changes of air into fire as the generation of Hephæstus, so, with the Egyptians, Osiris uniting with Isis (earth) is Neilos, and Typhon is the sea, into which Neilos falling vanishes and is dispersed, except such part [of him] as the earth takes up and receives, and so becomes endowed with productiveness by him.

3. And there is a sacred dirge made on Kronos[1]—and it laments "him who is born in the left-hand and died in the right-hand parts".

4. For Egyptians think that the eastern [parts] of cosmos are "face", the northern "right hand", and the southern "left hand".

5. The Nile, accordingly, since it flows from the southern [parts] and is consumed by the sea in the northern, is naturally said to have its birth in the left hand and its death in the right hand.

6. Wherefore the priests both pronounce the sea expiate and call salt "Typhon's foam"; and one of the chief prohibitions they have is: "Not to set salt on table." And they do not give greeting to sailors,[2] because they use the sea, and get their living from it. And for this cause chiefly they accuse fish of being a cause of offence, and write up: "Hate fish!"

7. At any rate at Saïs, in the entrance of the temple of Athena, there used to be chiselled up "babe", "old man", and after that "hawk", then "fish", and last of all "hippopotamus".

8. This meant in symbols: "O ye who are being born and are dying, God hates shamelessness."

9. For "babe" is the symbol of birth, and "old man" of death, and by "hawk" they mean God, and by "fish" hatred—as has been said on account of the sea—and by "hippopotamus" shamelessness, for it is fabled that after it has killed its sire it violates its dam.

10. Moreover, what is said by the Pythagorics, namely, that the sea is the tears of Kronos, would seem to riddle the fact of its not being pure and cognate with itself.

11. Let these things then be stated from outside sources as matters of common information.

XXXIII. 1. But the more wise of the priests call not only the Nile Osiris, and the sea Typhon; but [they call] without exception every source and power that moistens, Osiris—considering [him] cause of

---

[1] That is Nile.
[2] Lit., "pilots"; but presumably here used in a more general sense.

THE MYSTERIES OF ISIS AND OSIRIS

generation and essence of seed, and Typhon everything dry and fiery, and of a drying nature generally and one hostile to moisture.

2. And for this cause also, as they think he [Typhon] was born with a reddish-yellow body, somewhat pale, they do not by any means readily meet or willingly associate with men that look like this.

3. On the other hand, again, they say in the language of myth that Osiris was born black, because all [Nile] water blackens both earth and garments and clouds when mixed [with them], and [because] moisture in the young makes their hair black, whereas greyness comes on those past their prime, as though it were a turning pale owing to its drying up.

4. The spring, too, is blooming and productive and balmy; but autumn, through lack of moisture, is inimical to plants and baneful to animals.

5. And the ox that is kept at Sun-city which they call Mnevis—sacred to Osiris, while some also consider it sire of Apis—is black [also] and has second honours after Apis.

6. Moreover, they call Egypt, since it is especially black-soiled, just like the black of the eye, Chēmia, and liken it to a heart; for it is warm and moist, and is mostly confined in, and adjacent to, the southern part of the civilised world, just like the heart [is] in man's left-hand side.

XXXIV. 1. Moreover, they say that sun and moon do not use chariots for vehicles, but sail round in boats—[thus] riddling their being nourished by and being born in the "Moist".

2. And they think that Homer also, like Thales, set down Water as source and birth of all things, after learning [it] from Egyptians; for that Oceanus is Osiris, and Tēthys[1] Isis, as nursing all things and rearing them all up together.

3. For Greeks also call "emission of seed" ἀπ-ουσίαν and "intercourse" ἀυν-ουσίαν, and "son" (υἱὸν) from "water" (ὕδατος) and "moisten" (ὕσαι);[2] and [they call] Dionysus Huēs, as lord of the Moist Nature, in that he is no other than Osiris.

4. In fact, Hellanicus[3] seems to have heard Osiris called Hu-siris by the priests; for he persists in thus calling the god, presumably from his nature and power of invention.[4]

---
[1] As connected with Τήθη, the Nurse of all, and identified by some with the Primal Earth; and so signified by the word-play Τηθὺν and τιθην-ουμένην ("nursing").
[2] The word-play runs: ap-*ous*-ia, sun-*ous*-ia, hu-ion, hud-atos, hus-ai.
[3] The most eminent of the Greek logographers; fl. 553-504 B.C.
[4] εὑρέσεως—probably another word-play, *heuresis* and *husiris*.

215

CONCERNING OSIRIS AND DIONYSUS

XXXV. 1. That, however, he is the same as Dionysus—who should know better than thou thyself, O Klea, who art Archi-charila[1] of the Thyiades at Delphi, and wast dedicated to the Osiriaca before thou wert born?[2]

But if for the sake of others we must quote testimonies, let us leave the things that must not be spoken of in their proper place.

2. The rites, however, which the priests perform in burning the Apis, when they transport its body on a raft, in no way fall short of a Bacchic Orgy. For they put on fawn-skins and carry thyrsuses,[3] and shout and dance just like those inspired at celebrations of the Mysteries of Dionysus.

3. Wherefore many of the Greeks make Dionysus also bull-formed; while the women of the Eleians invoke him praying "the god with the bull's foot to come" to them.

4. The Argives, moreover, give Dionysus the epithet of "bull-born", and they call him up out of the water with the sound of trumpets, casting a lamb into the abyss for the Gate-keeper.[4] The trumpets they hide in thyrsi, as Socrates has said in his "[Books] on Rites".[5]

5. The Titanic [Passions] also and the [Dionysian] Night-rites agree with what we are told about the tearings-in-pieces and revivings and *palingeneses* of Osiris; and similarly the [stories] of the burials.

6. For both Egyptians point to tombs of Osiris everywhere, as has

---

[1] The text reads ἀρχικλά—an apparently impossible collection of letters. As no one has so far purged the reading, I would suggest χάριλαν or ἀρχι-χάριλαν. Stending (in Roscher, *s.v.*) reminds us of the myth of the orphan maid Charila, who during a famine begged alms at the gate of the palace of the King of ancient Delphi; the King not only refused her, but drove her away, slapping her face with his shoe. Whereupon the little maid for shame hanged herself. After the famine was over the Oracle decreed an atonement for her death. And so every nine years an effigy made to represent Charila was done to death, and then carried off by the leader of the Thyiades (or priestesses of Bacchus), and buried, with a rope round its neck, in a gorge. *Cf.* Harrison (Jane E.), *Prolegomena to the Study of Greek Religion* (Cambridge, 1903), p. 106. As Klea was leader of the Thyiades, this office fell to her; it may, therefore, even be that her name is some play on Charila.

[2] Lit., "from father and mother".

[3] Symbolic wands, generally cane-like or knotted like a bamboo, and sometimes wreathed in ivy and vine leaves, with a pine-cone at top.

[4] τῷ πυλαόχῳ.

[5] Müller, iv, 498. This was probably Socrates of Cos, who is known to have been the author of a work entitled Ἐπικλήσεις θεῶν (*e.g.* Dion. Laërt., ii, 4), meaning either "Prayers to the Gods", or "Surnames of the Gods".

THE MYSTERIES OF ISIS AND OSIRIS

been said,[1] and [also] Delphians believe the relics of Dionysus are deposited with them by the side of the Oracle, and the Holy Ones offer an offering, of which we must not speak, in the fane of Apollo, when the Thyiades awake "Him of the winnowing fan".

7. And that Greeks consider Dionysus to be lord and prince not only of wine, but of every moist nature, Pindar witnesses sufficiently when he sings:

> May gladsome Dionysus make the pasturage of trees to grow—
> Pure light of autumn.[2]

8. For which cause also they who give worship to Osiris are forbidden to destroy a cultivated tree or to stop up a water-source.

THE THEORY OF THE PHYSICISTS RESUMED

XXXVI. 1. And they call not only the Nile, but also without distinction all that is moist, "Osiris' efflux"; and the water-vase always heads the processions of the priests in honour of the God.

2. And with "rush"[3] they write "king" and the "southern climate" of the cosmos; and "rush" is interpreted as "watering" and "conception" of all things, and is supposed to resemble in its nature the generative member.

3. And when they keep the feast Pamylia, which is phallic, as has been said,[4] they bring out and carry round an image having a phallus three times the size of it.

4. For God is source, and every source by the power of generation makes manifold that which comes from it. And "many times" we are accustomed to call "thrice", as, for instance, "thrice-blessed", and "three times as many, endless, bonds"[5]—unless, indeed, "three fold" was used in its authentic meaning by those of old; for the Moist Nature, as being source and genesis of all, moved from the beginning the first three bodies—earth, air, and fire.

5. For the *logos* that is superadded to the myth—how that Typhon cast the chief part of Osiris into the river, and Isis could not find it, but after dedicating an object answering to it, and having made it ready, she commanded them to keep the Phallephoria in its honour

---

[1] *Cf.* xx, 5.
[2] Bergk, i, 433.
[3] θρύον—confounded by King (*in loc.*) with θρῖον, "fig leaf" (perhaps connected with τρίς, from the three lobes of the leaf); the "rush" is presumably the papyrus.
[4] *Cf.* xii.
[5] Bernardakis gives the references as *Il.*, vi, 154, and viii, 340, but I am unable to verify them.

—comes to this: namely, an instruction that the generative and spermatic [powers] of the God had moisture as their first matter, and by means of moisture were immingled with those things which have been produced to share in genesis.

6. But there is another *logos* of the Egyptians—that Apophis, as brother of the Sun, made war on Zeus, and that when Osiris fought on his [Zeus'] side and helped him to conquer his foe, Zeus adopted him as his son and called him Dionysus.

7. Moreover, the mythical nature of this *logos* goes to show that it connects with the truth about nature. For Egyptians call [Cosmic] Breath[1] Zeus—to which Dry and Fiery is hostile; this [latter] is not the Sun, but it has a certain kinship with him. And Moisture, by quenching the excess of Dryness, increases and strengthens the exhalations by which the Breath nourishes itself and waxes strong.

XXXVII. 1. Moreover, both Greeks consecrate the ivy to Dionysus and [also] among Egyptians it is said to be called *chen-osiris*—the name meaning, they say, "Osiris-plant".

2. Further, Ariston, who wrote *Colonies of the Athenians*, came across some Letter or other of Alexarchus's,[2] in which it is related that Dionysus, as son of Osiris and Isis, is not called Osiris but Arsaphēs by the Egyptians—([this is] in Ariston's first book)—the name signifying "manliness".

3. Hermæus also supports this in the first book of his *Concerning the Egyptians*, for he says that "Osiris" is, when translated, "Strong".[3]

4. I disregard Mnaseas,[4] who associated Dionysus and Osiris and Sarapis with Epaphos;[5] I also disregard Anticleides,[6] who says that Isis, as daughter of Prometheus,[7] lived with Dionysus; for the peculiarities which have been stated about the festivals and offerings carry a conviction with them that is clearer than the witnesses [I have produced].

XXXVIII. 1. And of the stars they consider Sirius to be Isis's[8]—as being a water-bringer. And they honour the Lion, and ornament

---

[1] Or "Spirit" ($\pi\nu\epsilon\hat{\upsilon}\mu\alpha$).

[2] Ariston and Alexarchus and Hermæus (*cf.* xlii, 7) seem to be otherwise unknown to fame.

[3] $\ddot{o}\mu\beta\rho\iota\mu\rho\varsigma=\ddot{o}\beta\rho\iota\mu\rho\varsigma$—strong, virile, manly. *Cf.* the Eleusinian sacred name Brimos for Iacchos.

[4] Flourished latter half of third century B.C.

[5] Son of Zeus and Io, born in the Nile, after the long wanderings of his mother. He is fabled by the Greeks to have been subsequently King of Egypt and to have built Memphis. Herodotus (ii, 153; iii, 27, 28) says that Epaphos = Apis.

[6] A Greek writer subsequent to the time of Alexander the Great.

[7] *Cf.* iii, 1.   [8] But *cf.* lxi, 5.

the doors of the temples with gaping lions' mouths; since Nilus overflows:

When first the Sun doth with the Lion join.[1]

2. And as they hold the Nile to be "Osiris's efflux", so, too, they think earth Isis's body—not all [of it], but what the Nile covers, sowing [her] with seed and mingling with her; and from this intercourse they give birth to Horus.

3. And Horus is the season *(ὥρα)* and [fair] blend of air that keeps and nourishes all in the atmosphere—who, they say, was nursed by Lētō in the marshes round Butō; for the watery and soaked-through earth especially nourishes the exhalations that quench and abate dryness and drought.

4. And they call the extremities of the land, both on the borders and where touching the sea, Nephthys; for which cause they give Nephthys the name of "End",[2] and say she lives with Typhon.

5. And when the Nile exceeds its boundaries and overflows more than usual, and [so] consorts with the extreme districts, they call it the union of Osiris with Nephthys—proof of which is given by the springing up of plants, and especially of the honey-clover,[3] for it was by its falling [from Osiris] and being left behind that Typhon was made aware of the wrong done to his bed. Hence it is that Isis conceived Horus in lawful wedlock, but Nephthys Anubis clandestinely.

6. In the Successions of the Kings,[4] however, they record that when Nephthys was married to Typhon, she was at first barren; and if they mean this to apply not to a woman but to their Goddess, they enigmatically refer to the utterly unproductive nature of the land owing to sterility.

XXXIX. 1. The conspiracy and despotism of Typhon, moreover, was the power of drought getting the mastery over and dispersing the moisture which both generates the Nile and increases it.

2. While his helper, the Æthiopian queen,[5] riddles southerly winds from Æthiopia. For when these prevail over the Annuals[6] (which drive the clouds towards Æthiopia), and prevent the rains which swell the Nile from bursting—Typhon takes possession and scorches; and thus entirely mastering the Nile he forces him out into the sea, contracted into himself through weakness and flowing empty and low.

---

[1] Aratus, *Phænom.*, 351. [2] *Cf.* xii, 6. [3] *Cf.* xiv, 6. [4] *Cf.* xi, 4. [5] Asō; *cf.* xiii, 3.
[6] The "Etesian" winds, which in Egypt blew from the N.W. during the whole summer.

3. For the fabled shutting-up of Osiris into the coffin is, perhaps, nothing but a riddle of the occultation and disappearance of water. Wherefore they say that Osiris disappeared in the mouth of Athyr[1]—when, the Annuals ceasing entirely, the Nile sinks, and the land is denuded, and, night lengthening, darkness increases, and the power of the light wanes and is mastered, and the priests perform both other melancholy rites, and, covering a cow made entirely of gold[2] with a black coat of fine linen as a mask of mourning for the Goddess—for they look on the "cow" as an image of Isis and as the earth—they exhibit it for four days from the seventeenth consecutively.

4. For the things mourned for are four: first, the Nile failing and sinking; second, the northern winds being completely extinguished by the southern gaining the mastery; third, the day becoming less than the night; and, finally, the denudation of the earth, together with the stripping of the trees which shed their leaves at that time.

5. And on the nineteenth, at night they go down to the sea; and the keepers and priests carry out the sacred chest, having within it a small golden vessel, into which they take and pour fresh water; and shouts are raised by the assistants as though Osiris were found.

6. Afterwards they knead productive soil with the water, and mixing with it sweet spices and fragrant incense, they mould it into a little moon-shaped image of very costly stuffs. And they dress it up and deck it out—showing that they consider these Gods the essence of earth and water.

XL. 1. And when again Isis recovers Osiris and makes Horus grow, strengthened with exhalations and moist clouds—Typhon is indeed mastered, but not destroyed.

2. For the Mistress and Goddess of the earth did not allow the nature which is the opposite of moisture to be destroyed entirely, but she slackened and weakened it, wishing that the blend should continue; for it was not possible the cosmos should be perfect, had the fiery [principle] ceased and disappeared.

3. And if these things are not said contrary to probability, it is probable also that one need not reject that *logos* also—how that Typhon of old got possession of the share of Osiris; for Egypt was [once] sea.[3]

---

[1] Copt. Hathor—corr. roughly with November.
[2] *Cf.* "the golden calf" incident of the Exodus story.
[3] Another proof of the common persuasion that there had been a Flood in Egypt.

THE MYSTERIES OF ISIS AND OSIRIS

4. For which cause many [spots] in its mines and mountains are found even to this day to contain shells; and all springs and all wells—and there are great numbers of them—have brackish and bitter water, as though it were the stale residue of the old-time sea collecting together into them.

5. But Horus in time got the better of Typhon—that is, a good season of rains setting in, the Nile driving out the sea made the plain reappear by filling it up again with its deposits—a fact, indeed, to which our senses bear witness; for we see even now that as the river brings down fresh mud, and advances the land little by little, the deep water gradually diminishes, and the sea recedes through its bottom being heightened by the deposits.

6. Moreover, [we see] Pharos, which Homer[1] knew as a day's sail distant from Egypt, now part [and parcel] of it; not that the [island] itself has sailed to land,[2] or extended itself shorewards, but because the intervening sea has been forced back by the river's reshaping of and adding to the mainland.

7. These [explanations], moreover, resemble the theological dogmas laid down by the Stoics—for they also say that the generative and nutritive Breath [or Spirit] is Dionysus; the percussive and separative, Heracles; the receptive, Ammon [Zeus]; that which extends through earth and fruits, Demeter and Korē; and that [which extends] through sea, Poseidon.[3]

THE THEORY OF THE MATHEMATICI

XLI. 1. Those, however, who combine with the above [considerations] of the Physicists some of the Mathematic [doctrines] derived from star-lore, think that the solar cosmos is called Typhon and the lunar Osiris.[4]

2. For [they think] that the Moon, in that its light is generative and moistening, is favourable both for breedings of animals and sproutings of plants; whereas the Sun, with untempered and harsh fire, burns and withers up [all] that are growing and blowing, and with fiery heat renders the major part of the earth entirely uninhabitable, and in many places utterly masters the Moon.

[1] *Il.*, iv, 355.
[2] A play on the "day's sail" (δρόμον) and ἀνα-δραμοῦσαν.
[3] It is, of course, a very poor interpretation of the myth to talk only about floods and desert, sea and rain, etc. These are all facts illustrating the underlying truth, but they are not the real meaning.
[4] This is a worse guess than even that of the Physicists. *Cf.* li, 5.

3. For which cause Egyptians always call Typhon Sēth[1]—that is, "that which oppresses and constrains by force".

4. And they have a myth that Heracles is settled in the Sun and accompanies him in his revolutions, while Hermes does the same with the Moon.

5. For the [revolutions] of the Moon resemble works of reason (*logos*) and super-abundant wisdom, while those of the Sun are like penetrating strokes [given] with force and power.[2]

6. Moreover, the Stoics say that the sun is kept burning and nourished from the sea,[3] whereas to the Moon the waters of springs and lakes send up a sweet and mild exhalation.

XLII. 1. The Egyptian myth runs that the death of Osiris took place on the seventeenth, when the full-moon is most conspicuously at the full.

2. Wherefore the Pythagoreans call this day also "Interception",[4] and regard this number as expiable.

3. For the "sixteen" being square and the "eighteen" oblong[5]—which alone of plane numbers happen to have their perimeters equal to the areas contained by them[6]—the mean, "seventeen", coming between them, intercepts and divorces them from one another, and divides the ratio of "nine" to "eight"[7] by being cut into unequal intervals.

4. And eight-and-twenty is the number of years which some say Osiris lived, and others that he reigned;[8] for this is the number of the lights of the Moon, and it rolls out its own circle in this number of days.

5. And at what they call the Burials of Osiris they cut the tree-trunk and make it into a crescent-shaped coffin, because the Moon, when it approaches the Sun, becomes crescent-shaped and hides itself away.

6. And the tearing of Osiris into fourteen pieces they refer

---

[1] *Cf.* lxii, 2 *et al.*
[2] *Cf.* the Stoic attributes of Heracles in xl, 7.
[3] If this is intended for the Great Sea of Space, it would be credible.
[4] ἀντίφραξιν.
[5] Square and Oblong were two of the fundamental "pairs of opposites" among the Pythagoreans. *Cf.* xlviii, 5.

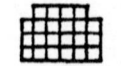

[7] The sesquioctave. In areas 8 is half of 16, and 9 of 18; while in a proportional measuring-rod or canon of 27 units, intervals of 8, 9, and 10 units succeeding one another complete the 27.
[8] *Cf.* xiii, 8, 9.

THE MYSTERIES OF ISIS AND OSIRIS

enigmatically to the days in which the luminary wanes after full-moon up to new-moon.

7. And the day on which it first appears, escaping from his beams and passing by the Sun, they call "Imperfect Good".

8. For Osiris is "Good-doer". The name, indeed, means many things, but chiefly what they call "Might energising and good-doing". And the other name of the God—Omphis, Hermæus[1] says, means [also] when translated, "Benefactor".

XLIII. 1. Moreover, they think that the risings of the Nile have a certain analogy with the lights of the Moon.

2. For the greatest [rising], about Elephantinē, is eight-and-twenty cubits, the same number as are the lights and measures of its monthly periods; and the least, about Mendes and Xoïs, is of six cubits, [analogous] to the half-moon; while the mean, about Memphis, when it is the right quantity, [is] of fourteen cubits, [analogous] to the full-moon.

3. And [they consider] the Apis the animated image of Osiris, and that he is conceived whenever generative light from the Moon fastens on a cow in heat.

4. For which cause also many of the markings of the Apis—lights shading off into darks—resemble the configurations of the moon.

5. Moreover, on the new-moon of the month Phamenōth[2] they keep festival, calling it "Entrance"[3] of Osiris into the Moon, as it is the beginning of spring.

6. By thus placing the power of Osiris in the Moon, they mean that Isis consorts with him while being [at the same time] the cause of his birth.[4]

7. For which cause also they call the Moon Mother of the cosmos, and think that she has a male-female nature—for she is filled by the Sun and made pregnant, and again of herself sends forth and disseminates into the air generative principles.

8. For [they say] she does not always overmaster the destruction wrought by Typhon;[5] but, though frequently mastered, even when bound hand and foot she frees herself again by her generative power, and fights the way through to Horus.

9. And Horus is the cosmos surrounding the earth—not entirely exempt from destruction either, nor yet from generation.

---

[1] *Cf.* xxxviii, 2.   [2] Copt. the same—roughly corr. to March.
[3] ἔμβασιν—or perhaps "Embarking".   [4] That is, is both wife and mother.
[5] Typhon being the Sun according to this theory.

XLIV. 1. Some, moreover, make out of the myth a riddle of the phenomena of eclipses also.

2. For the Moon is eclipsed at the full, when the Sun has the station opposite it, she entering the shadow of the earth—just as they say Osiris [entered] the coffin. And she again conceals the Sun and causes him to disappear, on the thirtieth [of the month], though she does not entirely destroy him, as neither did Isis Typhon.

3. And when Nephthys conceives Anubis, Isis adopts him. For Nephthys is that which is below the earth and non-manifest, while Isis [is] that which is above the earth and manifest.

4. And the circle just touching them and called "Horizon", as being common to both of them, has been called Anubis, and is likened to a dog for its characteristic; for the dog has the use of its sight both by day and night alike.

5. And Anubis seems to possess this power among Egyptians—just as Hecate with Greeks—being at one and the same time chthonian and olympian.[1]

6. Some, however, think that Anubis is Kronos;[2] wherefore as he breeds all things out of himself and conceives (κύων) [all] in himself, he got the name of Dog (κυών).

7. There is, then, for the worshippers of Anubis some [mystery] or other that may not be spoken of.[3]

8. In olden times, indeed, the dog enjoyed the highest honours in Egypt; but seeing that when Cambyses[4] slew the Apis and cast it out, no [animal] approached or touched its carcase but only the dog, he [thus] lost the [distinction of] being first and most honoured of the rest of the animals.

9. There are some, however, who call the shadow of the earth into which they think the Moon falls and is eclipsed, Typhon.

THE THEORY OF THE DUALISTS

XLV. 1. From [all of] which it seems not unreasonable to conclude that no simple [explanation] by itself gives the right meaning, but that they all collectively do so.

2. For neither drought nor wind nor sea nor darkness is the essential of Typhon, but the whole hurtful and destructive [element] which is in nature.

---

[1] That is, infernal and celestial. [2] In the sense of Time.
[3] This seems to suggest that Plutarch, though he faithfully records what "people say", by no means wishes his readers to believe them.
[4] But see xi, 4, and xxxi, 4.

THE MYSTERIES OF ISIS AND OSIRIS

3. For we must neither place the principles of the whole in soulless bodies, as [do] Democritus and Epicurus, nor yet assume one Reason (*Logos*) [only] and one Providence that prevails over and masters all things as demiurge [or artificer] of quality-less matter, as [do] the Stoics.

4. For it is impossible either that anything at all of no worth should exist where God is cause of all, or of worth where [He is cause] of nothing.

5. For "reciprocal" [is] cosmos' "harmony, as that of lyre or bow", according to Heracleitus,[1] and according to Euripides:

> There could not be apart good things and bad,
> But there's a blend of both so as to make things fair.[2]

6. Wherefore this exceedingly ancient doctrine also comes down from the theologers and law-givers to poets and philosophers—[a doctrine] that has its origin set down to no man's name, and yet possessed of credit, strong and not so easy to efface, surviving in many places not in words or voices[3] only, but also in [secret] perfectionings and [public] offerings, both non-Greek and Greek [ones] —that neither does the universe mindless and reason-less and guidance-less float in "That which acts of its own will", nor is there one Reason [only] that rules and guides, as though with rudder as it were and bits obedient to the reins; but that [the universe] is many things and these a blend of evil things and good.

7. Or, rather, seeing that Nature produces nothing, generally speaking, unmixed down here, it is not that from two jars a single mixer, like a tavern-keeper, pouring things out like drinks, mixes them up for us, but that from two opposite principles and two antagonistic powers—the one leading [things] to the right and on the straight [road], the other upsetting and undoing [them]—both life has been made mixed, and cosmos (if not the whole, at any rate this [cosmos] which surrounds the earth and comes after the Moon) irregular and variable, and susceptible of changes of every kind.

8. For if nothing has been naturally brought into existence without a cause, and Good cannot furnish cause of Bad, the nature of Bad as well as Good must have a genesis and principle peculiar to itself.

---

[1] Mullach, i, 319; Fairbanks (45), p. 37. The whole *logos* of Heracleitus runs: "They know not how differing agrees with itself—back-flying (παλίντονος) harmony as though of lyre or bow." That is, as a stretched string flies back again to its original position.

[2] Nauck, p. 294.

[3] That is, presumably, "in *logoi* and voices from heaven".

XLVI.[1] 1. And this is the opinion of most of the most wise.

2. For some think there are two craft-rival Gods, as it were—one the artificer of good [things], the other of [things] worthless. Others call the better "God" and the other "Daimon", as Zoroaster the Mage, who, they tell us, lived five thousand years before the Trojan War.

3. Zoroaster, then, called the one Ōromazēs, and the other Areimanios, and further announced that the one resembled light especially of things sensible, and the other, contrariwise, darkness and ignorance, while that between the two was Mithrēs; wherefore the Persians call Mithrēs the Mediator.

4. He taught them, moreover, to make offerings of gladsome prayers to the one, and to the other of melancholy de-precations.

5. For bruising a certain plant called "moly"[2] in a mortar, they invoke Hades and Darkness; then mixing it with the blood of a wolf whose throat has been cut, they carry it away and cast it into a sunless spot.

6. For they think that both of plants some are of the Good God and others of the Evil Daimon; and of animals, dogs, for instance, and birds[3] and hedgehogs of the Good, and water-rats of the Bad; wherefore they consider fortunate the man who kills the largest number [of the last].

XLVII. 1. Not that they also do not tell many mythic stories about the Gods; such as are, for example, the following:

Ōromazēs, born from the purest light, and Areimanios, of the nether darkness, are at war with one another.

2. And the former made six Gods: the first of good mind, the second of truth, the third of good order, and of the rest, one of wisdom, one of wealth, and the producer of things sweet following things fair; while the latter [made] craft-rivals as it were to those equal in number.

3. Then Ōromazēs having tripled himself, removed himself from the sun so far as the sun is distant from the earth, and adorned the heaven with stars; and he established one star above all as warder and look-out, [namely] Sirius.

4. And having made four-and-twenty other gods, he put them into an egg.

[1] For a criticism and notes on this chapter and the following, see Cumont (F.), *Textes et Monuments Figurés relatifs aux Mystères de Mithra* (Bruxelles, 1896), ii, 33-35.
[2] Thought by some to be the Cappadocian equivalent of the *haoma* or *soma* plant.
[3] That is "cocks".

THE MYSTERIES OF ISIS AND OSIRIS

Whereupon those that were made from Areimanios, just the same in number, piercing through the egg . . .[1]—whence the bad have been mingled with the good.

5. But a time appointed by Fate will come when Areimanios's letting loose of pestilence and famine must be utterly brought to an end, and made to vanish by these [good gods], and the earth becoming plane and level, there must ensue one mode of life and one way of government for men, all being happy and one-tongued.[2]

6. Theopompus, however, says that, according to the Magi, for three thousand years alternately one of the Gods conquers and the other is conquered, and for yet another three thousand years they fight and war, and each undoes the work of the other.

7. But that in the end Hades fails, and men shall be happy, neither requiring food nor casting shadow;[3] while the God who has contrived these things is still and at rest for a time—not otherwise long for a God, but proportionate to a man's sleeping.

8. The style of myth among the Magi, then, is somewhat after this manner.

XLVIII. 1. Moreover, Chaldæans declare that of the planets—which they call birth-presiding gods—two are good workers, two ill-doers, while three are intermediates and common.

2. As for the dogmas of the Greeks, they are, I take it, plain to all, ascribing as they do the good allotment to Olympian Zeus, and that which has to be averted to Hades.

3. Moreover, they have a myth that Harmony is the child of Aphrodite and Ares, the latter of whom is harsh and strife-loving, while the former is gentle and a lover of love-striving.

4. For Heracleitus plainly calls "War"—"father and king and lord of all",[4] and says that Homer, when he prays "that strife and hatred cease from gods as well",[5] forgets that he is imprecating the

---

[1] A *lacuna* occurs here in the text.
[2] This may refer to the consciousness of the spiritual life.
[3] There are thus three thousand years in which Ahura Mazda has the upper hand, three thousand in which Ahriman is victorious, three thousand in which the forces are balanced, and in the tenth thousand years comes the Day of Light. *Cf. Pistis Sophia*, 243: "Jesus answered and said unto Mary: 'A Day of Light is a thousand years in the world, so that thirty-six myriads of years and a half myriad of years of the world make a single Year of Light.'" The not casting of a shadow was supposed to be a characteristic of souls not attached to body; but it refers here rather to those who are "straight" with the Spiritual Sun.
[4] Fairbanks, (44) pp. 34, 35.
[5] *Cf. Il.*, xviii, 107; Fairbanks, (43) pp. 34, 35.

means of birth of all, in that they have their genesis from conflict and antipathy; that:

"Sun will not o'erstep his proper bounds, for if he do, Furies, Right's bodyguard, will find him out."[1]

5. The Pythagorics [also], in a list of names, set down the predicates of Good as—One, Finite, Abiding, Straight, Odd, Square, Equal, Right, Light; and of Bad as—Two, Infinite, Moving, Curved, Even, Oblong, Unequal, Left, Dark—on the ground that these are the underlying principles of genesis.

6. Aristotle [also predicates] the former as Form and the latter as Privation.

7. While Plato, though in many passages disguising himself and hiding his face, calls the former of the opposite principles Same and the latter Other.

8. But in his *Laws*, being now older, no longer in riddles and in symbols, but with authentic names, he says[2] cosmos is moved not by one soul, but probably by several, in any case not less than two—whereof the one is good-doing, the other the opposite to this and maker of things opposite.

9. He leaves out, however, a certain third intermediate nature, neither soul-less nor reason-less nor motion-less of itself, as some think,[3] but depending on both of them, and for ever longing for and desiring and following after the better, as the following [passages] of the argument (*logos*),[4] combining as it does for the most part the theology of the Egyptians with their philosophy, show.

XLIX. 1. For though the genesis and composition of this cosmos has been blended from opposing, though not equal-strengthed, powers, the lordship is nevertheless that of the Better [one].

2. Still it is impossible the Worse should be entirely destroyed, as it is largely innate in the body and largely in the soul of the universe, and ever in desperate conflict with the Better.

3. In the Soul [of cosmos], then, Mind and Reason (*Logos*), the guide and lord of all the best in it, is Osiris; and so in earth and air and water and heaven and stars, that which is ordered and appointed and in health, is the efflux of Osiris, reflected in seasons and temperatures and periods.

---

[1] Fairbanks, (29) pp. 32, 33.
[2] This is a very brief summary of the argument in *Legg.*, x, 896 ff. (Jowett, v, 282 ff.).
[3] *Cf.* xlv, 6.
[4] This "argument" is Plutarch's own treatise and not Plato's dialogue, as King supposes.

THE MYSTERIES OF ISIS AND OSIRIS

4. But Typhon is the passionate and titanic and reasonless and impulsive [aspect] of the Soul, while of its corporeal [side he is] the death-dealing and pestilent and disturbing, with unseasonable times and intemperate atmospheres and concealments of sun and moon—as though they were the charges and obliterations of Typhon.

5. And the name is a predicate of Sēth, as they call Typhon; for [Sēth] means "that which oppresses and constrains by force";[1] it means also, frequently, "turning upside down", and, again, "overleaping".

6. Some, moreover, say that one of the companions of Typhon was Bebōn;[2] while Manethōs [says] that Typhon himself was also called Bebōn, and that the name signifies "holding back" or "hindering", since the power of Typhon stands in the way of things going on their way and moving towards what they have to.

L. 1. Wherefore also of domestic animals they apportion to him the least tractable—the ass; while of wild ones, the most savage—the crocodile and hippopotamus.

2. As to the ass, we have already given some explanation. At Hermes-city, however, as image of Typhon, they show us a hippopotamus on which stands a hawk[3] fighting a snake—indicating by the hippopotamus Typhon, and by the hawk power and rule, of which Typhon frequently possessing himself by force, ceases not from being himself in and throwing [others] into a state of disorder by means of evil.

3. Wherefore also when they make offerings on the seventh of the month Tybi[4]—which [day] they call "Arrival of Isis from Phœnicia", they mould on the cakes a bound hippopotamus.[5]

4. And at Apollo-city it is the custom for absolutely everyone to eat a piece of crocodile. And on one [particular] day they hunt down and kill as many [of them] as they possibly can, and throw them down right in front of the temple, saying that Typhon escaped Horus by turning himself into a crocodile—considering as they do that all animals and plants and experiences that are evil and harmful are Typhon's works and parts and movements.

LI. 1. Osiris, again, on the other hand, they write with "eye" and "sceptre",[6] the former of which [they say] shows his providence, and

---

[1] *Cf.* xli, 2.
[2] βέβωνα, but perhaps rather βεβῶνα—and so βεβῶς, a play on βεβῶν, "steadying" or "straining". In Eg. Bebi or Baba; *cf.* Budge, *op. cit.*, ii, 92.
[3] *Cf.* li, 2.   [4] Copt. Tobi—corr. roughly to January.
[5] *Cf.* "bound ass" above, xxx, 3.   [6] *Cf.* x, 6.

the latter his power; just as Homer, when calling him who is ruler and king of all "Zeus supreme counsellor",[1] seems by "supreme" to signify his supremacy, and by "counsellor" his good counsel and providence.

2. They frequently write this god with "hawk"[2] as well; for it excels in tension of sight and swiftness of flight, and can naturally support itself on the smallest quantity of food.

3. It is said, moreover, to hover over the bodies of the unburied dead and to cast earth upon them.[3] And when it drops down on the river to drink, it sets its wings upright, and after drinking it lowers them again—by which it is evident it saves itself and escapes from the crocodile, for if it is caught its wings remain fixed as they were set.[4]

4. And everywhere they exhibit a man-shaped image of Osiris—ithyphallic, because of his generative and luxuriant [nature].

And they dress his statue in a flame-coloured robe—since they consider the sun as body of the power of the Good, as it were a visible [sign] of an essence that mind only can conceive.

5. Wherefore also we should pay no attention to those who assign the sphere of the sun to Typhon[5]—to whom nothing light or salutary, neither order nor genesis, nor any motion that has measure and reason, belongs, but [rather] their contraries.

6. And we should not set down drought which destroys many of the animals and plants, as the sun's work, but [rather as that] of the breaths and waters in earth and air not being seasonably blended when the principle of disorderly and unbounded power makes discord and quenches the exhalations.

LII. 1. And in the sacred hymns to Osiris, they invoke him who is hidden in the Arms of the Sun;[6] and on the thirteenth of the month of Epiphi[7] they keep with feast the Birthday of the Eye of Horus, when moon and sun are in the same straight line; as they think that not only the moon but also the sun is eye and light of Horus.

2. And on the eighth of the waning [half] of Paōphi[8] they keep the Birthday of the Sun's Staff, after the autumnal equinox—signifying

---

[1] *Il.*, viii, 22; xvii, 339. [2] *Cf.* l, 2. Compare the Eagle of Zeus.
[3] More of the "Physiologus".
[4] "In the crocodile's gullet," comments King, "and so prevents him gulping down the bird." We are, however, inclined to think that Plutarch is a bit of a humourist, and that there is no necessity for commenting seriously on his *on dits*.
[5] *Cf.* xli, 1; also § 9 below. [6] That is the Sun's Rays.
[7] Copt. Epep—corr. roughly with July.
[8] Copt. Paopi—corr. roughly with October.

THE MYSTERIES OF ISIS AND OSIRIS

that he needs an underprop, as it were, and strengthening, deficient as he is in heat and light, declining and moving obliquely from us.

3. Moreover, just after the winter solstice they carry the Cow round the shrine [seven times], and the circuit is called the Seeking for Osiris, as in winter the Goddess longs for the "water" of the Sun.

4. And she goes round this number of times, because he completes his passing from the winter to the summer solstice in the seventh month.

5. Moreover, Horus, son of Osiris, is said to have been the first of all to make offerings to the Sun on the fourth of the waxing moon, as is written in the [books] entitled *Birthdays of Horus*.

6. Though indeed every day they offer incense to the Sun in three kinds—resin at his rising, myrrh at mid-heaven, and what is called "kuphi" at his setting; the reason for each of which I will explain later on.[1] And with all these they think to make the Sun propitious to them and to do him service.

7. But what need is there to collect many such indications? For there are those who say point-blank that Osiris is Sun and is called Sirius by Greeks—though with Egyptians the addition of the article has caused the name to be mistaken[2]—and who declare Isis to be no other than Moon; whence also [they say] that the horned ones of her statues are representations of her crescent, while by the black-robed ones are signified the occultations and overshadowings in which she follows Sun longing after him.

8. Accordingly they invoke Moon for affairs of love; and Eudoxus[3] says that Isis decides love-affairs.

9. And these [explanations] have in a modified way some share of plausibility; whereas it is not worth while even listening to those who make the Sun Typhon.

10. But let us ourselves again take up the proper reason (*logos*).

THE PROPER REASON ACCORDING TO PLUTARCH

LIII. 1. For Isis is the feminine [principle] of Nature and that which is capable of receiving the whole of genesis; in virtue of which she has been called "Nurse" and "All-receiving" by Plato,[4] and, by the

---

[1] *Cf.* lxxix, lxxx.
[2] That is ὁ σείριος = ὅσιρις—an absurd contention, of course, though flattering to Greek vanity.
[3] *Cf.* vi, x, xxx, lxii, lxiv.   [4] *Timæus*, 51 A.

multitude, "She of ten-thousand names", through her being transformed by Reason (*Logos*) and receiving all forms and ideas [or shapes].

2. And she hath an innate love of the First and Most Holy of all things (which is identical with the Good), and longs after and pursues it. But she flees from and repels the domain of the Bad, and though she is the field and matter of them both, yet doth she ever incline to the Better of herself, and offers [herself] for him to beget and sow into herself emanations and likenesses, with which she joys and delights that she is pregnant and big with their generations.

3. For Generation is image of Essence in Matter and Becoming copy of Being.

LIV. 1. Hence not unreasonably do they say in the myth that [while] the Soul of Osiris is eternal and indestructible, Typhon often tears his Body in pieces and makes it disappear, and that Isis seeks it wandering and puts it together again.

2. For the Real and Conceivable-by-the-mind-alone and Good is superior to destruction and change; but the images which the sensible and corporeal imitates from it, and the reasons (*logoi*) and forms and likenesses which it receives, just as seal-impressions in wax, do not last for ever, but are seized upon by the disorderly and turbulent [elements], expelled hither from the field above, and fighting against the Horus whom Isis brings forth as the sensible image of that cosmos which mind alone can conceive.

3. Wherefore also [Horus] is said to have a charge of bastardy brought against him by Typhon—of not being pure and unalloyed like his sire, Reason (*Logos*), itself by itself, unmixed and impassible, but bastardised with matter on account of the corporeal [element].[1]

4. Nevertheless, Horus gets the best of it and wins, through Hermes—that is, the Reason (*Logos*)[2]—bearing witness and showing that Nature reflects the [true] Cosmos by changing her forms according to That-which-mind-alone-can-conceive.[3]

5. For the genesis of Apollo[4] from Isis and Osiris[5] that took place while the Gods were still in the womb of Rhea, is an enigmatical way of stating that before this [sensible] cosmos became manifest, and Matter was perfected by Reason (*Logos*), Nature, proving herself imperfect, of herself brought forth her first birth.

[1] *Cf. C. H.*, x (xi), 10; Lact., iv, 6 (Frag. v).
[2] This shows that in one tradition Hermes and Osiris were identified.
[3] *Cf.* xix, 4.   [4] *Sc.* Horus.
[5] The sequel I think shows that "and Osiris" is a gloss; but see xii, 8.

THE MYSTERIES OF ISIS AND OSIRIS

6. Wherefore also they say that that God was lame[1] in the dark, and call him Elder Horus; for he was not cosmos, but a sort of image and phantasm of the world which was to be.[2]

LV. 1. But this Horus [of ours] is their Son,[3] horizoned[4] and perfect, who has not destroyed Typhon utterly, but has brought over to his side his efficacy and strength; hence they say it is that the statue of Horus at Coptos grasps in one hand Typhon's *virilia*.

2. Moreover, they have a myth that Hermes cut out the sinews of Typhon and used them for lyre strings—[thus] teaching [us] how Reason (*Logos*) brought the universe into harmony, and made it concordant out of discordant elements. He did not destroy the destructive power but tamed it.

3. Hence while weak and ineffective up there, down here, by being blinded and interwoven with the passible and changeable elements, it is cause of shakings and tremors in earth, of droughts and tempests in air, and again of lightnings and thunderings.

4. Moreover, it infects waters and winds with pestilences, and shoots up and rears itself as far as the moon, frequently blurring and blackening its light, as Egyptians think.

5. And they say that Typhon at one time strikes the Eye of Horus, and at another takes it out and swallows it. By "striking" they refer enigmatically to the monthly diminution of the moon, and by "blinding" to its eclipse, which the sun remedies by immediately shining on it after it has passed out of the shadow of the earth.[5]

LVI. 1. Now the better and diviner Nature is from these:—[to wit] the Intelligible and Matter, and that from them which Greeks call Cosmos.

---

[1] *Cf.* lxii.

[2] These two paragraphs are, in my opinion, of the utmost value for the critical investigation of the sources of the famous Sophia-mythus of Gnosticism. The imperfect birth (Abortion) of the Sophia (Wisdom, Nature, Isis), as the result of her effort to bring forth of herself, without her consort, or syzygy, while still in the Plērōma (Womb of Rhea), paves the way for the whole scheme of one of the main forms of Gnostic cosmology and subsequent soteriology, the Creator Logos and Saviour having to perfect the imperfect product of Nature. This is, I believe, the first time that the above passage of Plutarch has been brought into connection with the Sophia-mythus, and all previous translations with which I am acquainted accordingly make havoc of the meaning. See F. F. F., pp. 339 ff.; and for the Pauline use of the technical term "Abortion", D. J. L., pp. 355 ff.; for "Balaam the Lame Man" (? a by-name for Jeschu-Horus), see *ibid.*, p. 201. Reitzenstein (pp. 39, 40) quotes these two chapters, and adds some parallels from the Trismegistic literature.

[3] Adopting the suggestion of Bernardakis—ὁ υἱός for αὐτός.

[4] Or "defined", ὡρισμένος—a play on ὧρος.

[5] All this according to the Mathematici, presumably; the "eye" of Horus would rather signify "mentality".

2. Plato,[1] indeed, was wont to call the Intelligible Idea and Model and Father; and Matter Mother and Nurse—both place and ground of Genesis; and the offspring of both Genesis.

3. And one might conjecture that Egyptians [also revered][2] the fairest of the triangles, likening the nature of the universe especially to this; for Plato also, in his *Republic*,[3] seems to have made additional use of this in drawing up his marriage scheme.[4]

4. And this triangle has its perpendicular [side] of "three", its base of "four", and its hypotenuse of "five"; its square being equal to the [sum of the] squares on the containing sides.[5]

5. We must, accordingly, compare its perpendicular to male, its base to female, and its hypotenuse to the offspring of both; and [conjecture] Osiris as source, Isis as receptacle, and Horus as result.

6. For the "three" is the first "odd"[6] and perfect;[7] while the "four" [is] square from side "even" two;[8] and the "five" resembles partly its father and partly its mother, being composed of "three" and "two".

7. And *panta* [all] is only a slight variant of *pente* [five]; and they call counting *pempasasthai* [reckoning by fives].

8. And five makes a square equal to the number of letters among Egyptians,[9] and a period of as many years as the Apis lives.

9. Thus they usually call Horus also Min[10]—that is, "being seen"; for cosmos is a sensible and see-able thing.

10. And Isis is sometimes called Muth,[11] and again Athyri[12] and Methyer. And by the first of the names they mean "Mother"; by

---

[1] *Timæus*, 50 C.   [2] There is a *lacuna* in the text.
[3] *Rep.*, 545 D ff. See also Adam (J.), *The Nuptial Number of Plato: its Solution and Significance* (London, 1891).
[4] That is to say, that in Plutarch's opinion Plato derived the idea originally from Egypt.
[5] That is $9+16=25$.   [6] "One" being reckoned neither odd nor even.
[7] That is, divisible by itself and "one" only.
[8] τετράγωνος ἀπὸ πλευρᾶς ἀρτίου τῆς δυάδος.
[9] That is, the Egyptian alphabet consisted of 25 letters.
[10] In the Ritual (chap. xvii, 30), the deceased is made to say: "I am the God Åmsu (or Min) in his coming forth; may his two plumes be set upon my head for me." And in answer to the question: "Who, then, is this?"—the text goes on to say: "Åmsu is Horus, the avenger of his father, and his coming forth is his birth. The plumes upon his head are Isis and Nephthys when they go forth to set themselves there, even as his protectors, and they provide that which his head lacketh; or (as others say), they are the two exceeding great uraei which are upon the head of their father Tem, or (as others say), his two eyes are the two plumes which are upon his head." (Budge, *op. cit.*, ii, 258.)
[11] Eg. Mut, the syzygy of Åmen. Mut means "Mother"; she was the Worldmother. See Budge, *op. cit.*, ii, 28 ff.
[12] *Cf.* lxix, 4, "Athyr" probably meaning Hathor.

THE MYSTERIES OF ISIS AND OSIRIS

the second, "Cosmic House" of Horus—as also Plato [calls her] "Ground of Genesis" and "She who receives"; and the third is compounded from "Full" and "Cause"—for Matter is full of Cosmos, and consorts with the Good and Pure and Ordered.

LVII. 1. And Hesiod[1] also, when he makes all the first [elements to be] Chaos and Earth and Tartarus and Love, might be thought to assume no other principles than these—if at any rate in substituting the names we assign to Isis that of Earth, to Osiris that of Love, and to Typhon that of Tartarus; for his Chaos seems to be subsumed as ground and place of the universe.

2. Our data also in a way invite as witness Plato's myth which Socrates details in the *Symposium*[2] about the Birth of Love—telling [us how] that Poverty wanting children lay down by the side of sleeping Means, and conceiving by him brought forth Love of a mixed nature and capable of assuming every shape, in as much, indeed, as he is the offspring of a good and wise father and one sufficient for all, but of an incapable mother and one without means,[3] who on account of her need is ever clinging to someone else and importuning someone else.[4]

3. For his Means is no other than the First Beloved and Desirable and Perfect and Sufficient; and he calls Matter Poverty—who is herself of herself deficient of the Good, but is ever being filled by Him and longing for and sharing in [Him].

4. And the Cosmos, that is Horus, is born from these; and Horus, though neither eternal nor impassible nor indestructible, but ever-generable, continues by means of the changes and periods of his passions to remain ever young and ever to escape destruction.

LVIII. 1. Now, we should make use of the myths not as though they were altogether sacred sermons (*logoi*), but taking the serviceable [element] of each according to its similitude [to reason].

2. When, then, we say Matter, we should not be swept into the opinions of some philosophers, and suppose some body or other of itself soul-less and quality-less, and inert and inefficient; for we call oil the "matter" of a perfume, [and] gold that of a statue, though they are not destitute of every quality.

3. [Nay,] we submit the soul itself and [even] the thought of man as the "matter" of knowledge and virtue to the reason (*logos*) to order and bring into rhythm.

---

[1] *Theog.*, 116–22.   [2] *Symp.*, 203 B; Jowett, i, 573 ff.
[3] ἀπόρον—a play on πόρος.   [4] *Cf.* lviii, 6, last clause.

4. Moreover, some have declared the mind [to be] "region of ideas", and, as it were, the "impressionable substance[1] of the intelligibles".

5. And some think that the substance of the woman[2] is neither power nor source, but matter and nutriment of birth.

6. If, then, we attach ourselves to these, we ought thus also to think of this Goddess as having eternally her share in the First God, and consorting [with Him] for love of the goodness and beauty that surround Him, never opposed to Him, but, just as we say that a lawful and righteous husband loves [his wife] righteously, and a good wife though she has her husband and consorts with him, still desires [him], so [should we] think of Her as clinging to Him, and importuning Him,[3] though [ever] filled full with His supremest and purest parts.

LIX. 1. But where Typhon steals in, laying hold of the last [parts, we should think of Her as] then seeming to wear a melancholy countenance, and being said to mourn, and to be seeking after certain relics and fragments of Osiris, and enfolding them in her robes, receiving them when destroyed into herself, and hiding them away, just as She also produces them again when they are born, and sends them forth from herself.

2. For while the reasons (*logoi*) and ideas and emanations of the God in heaven and stars remain [for ever], those that are disseminated into things passible—in earth and sea and plants and animals—being dissolved and destroyed and buried, come to light over and over again and reappear in their births.

3. For which cause the myth says that Typhon lived with Nephthys, but that Osiris had knowledge of her secretly.

4. For the last parts of Matter, which they call Nephthys and End, are mainly in possession of the destructive power; nevertheless the Generative and Saving One distributes into them weak and faint seed which is destroyed by Typhon, except so much as Isis by adoption saves and nourishes and compacts together.

LX. 1. But He is on the whole the Better one, as both Plato and Aristotle suppose; and the generative and moving [power] of Nature moves to Him and towards being, while the annihilating and destructive [moves] from Him and towards non-being.

---

[1] ἐκμαγεῖον. *Cf.* Plat., *Tim.*, 50 C; *Theæt.*, 191 C, 196 A.
[2] τὸ σπέρμα τῆς γυναικός—lit., "the seed of the woman".
[3] *Cf.* lvii, 2.

THE MYSTERIES OF ISIS AND OSIRIS

2. Wherefore they derive the name Isis from hastening (ἵεσθαι) and coursing with knowledge, since she is ensouled and prudent motion.

3. For her name is not foreign;[1] but just as all the Gods have a common name from two elements—"that which can be seen" and "that which runs"[2]—so *we* call this Goddess "Isis" from "knowledge",[3] and Egyptians [also] call her Isis.[4]

4. And thus Plato also says the ancients signified the "Holy[5] [Lady]" by calling her "Isia"—and so also "Mental Perception" and "Prudence", in as much as she is [the very] course and motion of Mind hastening[6] and coursing, and that they placed Understanding —in short, the Good and Virtue—in things that flow[7] and run.

5. Just as [he says] again, the Bad is railed at with corresponding names, when they call that which hinders nature and binds it up and holds it and prevents it from hastening and going, "badness",[8] "difficulty",[9] "cowardice"[10] [and] "distress".

LXI. 1. And Osiris has had his name from a combination of ὅσιος (holy) and ἱερός (sacred); for there is a common Reason (*Logos*) of things in Heaven and of things in Hades—the former of which the ancients were accustomed to call sacred, and the latter holy.

2. And the Reason that [both] brings [down] to light the heavenly things and is [also] of things that are mounting upwards,[11] is called Anubis, and sometimes also Hermanubis,[12] belonging in his former capacity to things above and in his latter to things below [them].

3. Wherefore also they offer him in his former capacity a white cock,[13] and in his latter a saffron-coloured one—thinking that the former things are pure and the latter mixed and manifold.

---

[1] That is, non-Greek—βαρβαρικόν. *Cf.* ii, 2.
[2] The word-play being θεός—θεατός—θέον.
[3] *Cf.* ii, 3, for the word-play, and also for ὁσία in the next paragraph.
[4] They, however, probably called her something resembling Åst.
[5] τὴν ὁσιάν—but Plutarch is mistaken, for in *Cratylus*, 401 C it is a question of οὐσιάν and ἐσιάν and not of ὁσιάν and ἰσίαν.
[6] ἱεμένου, picking up the ἵεσθαι above in paragraph 2.
[7] *Cf. Crat.*, 415 D, where the word-play is ἀρετή and ἀει-ρείτη (ever-flowing).
[8] *Cf. Crat.*, 415 C—where the play is κακ-ία=κακῶς ἰὸν (ἰέναι)—badly going.
[9] ἀπορ-ία—the word-play being ἀ (not) and πορ-εύεσθαι (going)—*ibid.*, C, D.
[10] "δειλία signifies that the soul is bound with a strong chain (δεσμός), for λίαν means strength, and therefore δειλία expresses the greatest and strongest bond of the soul" (*ibid*). See Jowett, i, 359 f.
[11] That is, things in Hades (the Invisible)—not Tartarus.
[12] Horus was endowed with many characteristics of other gods. Thus with Ånpu or Anubis he becomes Ḥeru-em-Ånpu, *i.e.* Horus as Anubis, and is said to dwell in the "divine hall". This is the Hermanubis of Plutarch. *Cf.* Budge, *op. cit.*, i, 493.
[13] "A cock to Æsculapius."

4. Nor ought we to be surprised at the manipulation of the names back into Greek.[1] For tens of thousands of others that disappeared with those who emigrated from Greece, continue unto this day and sojourn with foreigners; for recalling some of which they blame the poets' art as "barbarising"—I mean those who call such words "glosses".[2]

5. Further, they relate that in what are called the "Books of Hermes", it is written that they call the Power that rules the ordained revolution of the Sun, Horus, while the Greeks [call it] Apollo; and the Power that rules the Breath [or Spirit], some [call] Osiris, others Sarapis, and others Sōthis in Egyptian.

6. The last means "conception" *(κύησιν)* or "conceiving" *(τὸ κύειν)*.[3] Wherefore also, by inversion of the name, the star [Sōthis] which they consider the special one of Isis, is called Dog *(κύων)* in Greek.

7. We should, however, least of all be jealous about the names; still if we were, I would sooner give up "Sarapis" than "Osiris"; for though I think the former is a foreign one and the latter Greek, yet are they both [names] of One God and One Power.

LXII. 1. The Egyptian [names] also resemble these [Greek ones]. For they often call Isis by the name of Athena, which expresses some such meaning as "I have come from myself"—which is [again] indicative of self-motive course.

2. While "Typhon", as has been said,[4] is called Sēth and Bebōn and Smu—the names being intended to signify a certain forcible and preventative checking, opposition or reversing.

3. Moreover, they call the loadstone "Bone of Horus",[5] and iron "[Bone] of Typhon", as Manethōs relates; for just as iron often resembles that which is attracted to and follows after the loadstone, and often is turned away from it, and repelled to an opposite direction, so the saving and good and reason-possessing motion of the Cosmos both turns towards itself and makes more gentle by persuasion that harsh and typhonean [motion]; and then again after raising it into itself, it reverses it and plunges it into the infinitude.

4. Moreover, Eudoxus[6] says that the Egyptians tell a myth about

---

[1] *Cf.* xxix, 8.
[2] γλώττας—a technical term for obsolete or foreign words that need explanation.
[3] *Cf.* xxi, 2.
[4] *Cf.* xli, xlix (end).
[5] *Cf.* the "bone of the sea-hawk" in Hipp., *Philo.*, v, 9 and 17; and note to J., in "Myth of Man in the Mysteries", p. 189.
[6] *Cf.* xxx, lxix, *et al.*

THE MYSTERIES OF ISIS AND OSIRIS

Zeus that, as in consequence of his having his legs grown together,[1] he could not walk, for shame he lived in solitude; and so Isis, by cutting in two and separating these limbs of his body, made his going even-footed.[2]

5. By those things, moreover, the myth enigmatically hints that the Mind and Reason (*Logos*) of God after it had progressed[3] in itself in the invisible and unmanifest, came forth into genesis by means of motion.

THE SYMBOLISM OF THE SISTRUM

LXIII. 1. The sistrum (σεῖστρον) also shows that existent things must be shaken up (σείεσθαι) and never have cessation from impulse, but as it were be wakened up and agitated when they fall asleep and die away.

2. For they say they turn aside and beat off Typhon with sistra—signifying that when corruption binds nature fast and brings her to a stand, [then] generation frees her and raises her from death by means of motion.

3. Now the sistrum has a curved top, and its arch contains the four [things] that are shaken. For the part of the cosmos which is subject to generation and corruption, is circumscribed by the sphere of the moon, and all [things] in it are moved and changed by the four elements—fire and earth and water and air.

4. And on the arch of the sistrum, at the top, they put the metal figure of a cat with a human face, and at the bottom, below the shaken things, the face sometimes of Isis and sometimes of Nephthys—symbolising by the faces generation and consummation (for these are the changes and motions of the elements), and by the cat the moon, on account of the variable nature,[4] night habits, and fecundity of the beast.

5. For it is fabled to bring forth one, then two, and [then] three, and four, and five [at a birth], and then adds one by one until seven;[5]

---

[1] The invisible serpent-form of the God.

[2] *Cf.* Plat., *Tim.*, 44 D and 45 A; and liv, 5, above concerning the birth of the Elder Horus.

[3] Or "walked", suggesting some idea of single motion in itself—the motion of "sameness", symbolised by a serpent with its tail in its mouth. The serpent was one of the most favourite symbols of the Logos, and this perhaps accounts for the "legs grown together".

[4] τὸ ποικίλον. King translates this "pied colour", and deduces that "the original colour of the cat was tabby"; but, as the schoolboy says, I don't see it.

[5] More "Physiologus"; or rather, there was a mystical theory about other things which was adapted to a popular natural history of the cat, and then the fable was cited as "proof" of the original theory.

so that in all she brings forth eight-and-twenty, the number of lights of the moon.

6. This, however, is probably somewhat too mythical; anyway, the pupils of its eyes seem to become full and dilate at the full-moon, and to contract and shut out the light during the wanings of that luminary.

7. And by the human face of the cat is signified the intellectual and reasonable nature of the changes that take place in connection with the moon.

THE TRUE "LOGOS", AGAIN, ACCORDING TO PLUTARCH

LXIV. 1. But, to speak concisely, it is not correct to consider either water or sun or earth or heaven as Osiris or Isis, or, again, fire or drought or sea as Typhon; but if we were to assign simply that [nature] to the latter which is not subject to measure or rule owing to excesses or insufficiencies, and should reverence and honour that which has been subjected to order and is good and beneficent, as the work of Isis, and the image and copy and reason of Osiris, we should not miss the mark.

2. Moreover, we shall make Eudoxus[1] cease to disbelieve and be perplexed, how it is neither Demeter who has charge of love-affairs but Isis, nor Dionysus who has the power either to make the Nile increase or to rule over the dead [but Osiris].

3. For we think that by one Common Reason (*Logos*)[2] these Gods have been ordained over every domain of good; and every fair and good thing possible for nature owes its origin to their means—[Osiris] giving [them] their origins and [Isis] receiving and distributing [them].

AGAINST THE WEATHER AND VEGETATION GOD THEORIES

LXV. 1. And we shall also get our hands on the dull crowd who take pleasure in associating the [mystic recitals] about these Gods either with changes of the atmosphere according to the seasons, or with the generation of the corn and sowings and ploughings, and in saying that Osiris is buried when the sown corn is hidden by the earth, and comes to life and shows himself again when it begins to sprout.

---

[1] *Cf.* lxii, *et al.*
[2] Parallel to "Common Sense".

THE MYSTERIES OF ISIS AND OSIRIS

2. For which cause also [they declare] that Isis, on feeling she is pregnant, ties an amulet round her [neck] on the sixth day of the first half of the month Phaōphi;[1] and that Harpocrates is brought forth about the winter solstice imperfect and infant in the things that sprout too early.[2]

3. For which cause they offer him first-fruits of growing lentils, and they keep the days of thanks for safe delivery after the spring equinox.

4. For they love to hear these things and believe them, drawing conviction from things immediately at hand and customary.

LXVI. 1. Still there is nothing to complain of if [only], in the first place, they cherish the Gods in common with ourselves, and do not make them peculiar to Egyptians, either by characterising Nile and only the land that Nile waters by these names, or, by saying that marshes and lotuses and god-making [are their monopoly], deprive the rest of mankind who have no Nile or Butō or Memphis, of [the] Great Gods.

2. Indeed, all [men] have Isis and know her and the Gods of her company; for though they learned not long ago to call some of them by names known among the Egyptians, still they knew and honoured the power of each [of them] from the beginning.

3. In the second place, and what is more important—they should take very good heed and be apprehensive lest unwittingly they write-off the sacred mysteries and dissolve them into winds and streams, and sowing and ploughings, and passions of earth and changes of seasons.

4. As those who [say] that Dionysus is wine and Hephæstus flame, and Persephone, as Cleanthes says somewhere, the wind that drives through the crops and is killed; and [as] some poet says of the reapers:

Then when they, lusty, cut Demeter's limbs.[3]

5. For these in nothing differ from those who regard a pilot as sails and ropes and anchor, and a weaver as yarns and threads, and a physician as potions and honey-brew and barley-water; nay, they put into men's minds dangerous and atheistic notions, by transferring names of Gods to natures and to things that have no sense or

---

[1] Copt. Paopi—corr. roughly with October.
[2] *Cf.* lxviii, 2, 3. Ḥeru-p-Khart, Horus the Younger, or the "Child", so called to distinguish him from Ḥeru-ur, or Horus the Elder. *Cf.* Budge, *op. cit.*, i, 468 f.
[3] *Cf.* Ps. Plut., *De Vita Homeri*, § 23.

soul, and which are necessarily destroyed by men according to their need and use. For it is not possible to consider such things in themselves as Gods.

LXVII. 1. For a God is not a thing without a mind or soul, or one made subject to the hand of man; but it is from these things that we deduce that those who bestow them on us for our use and offer them [to us] in perpetual abundance, are Gods.

2. Not different [Gods] for different peoples, not non-Greek and Greek, not southern and northern [Gods]; but just as sun and moon and earth and sea [are] common to all [men], though they are called by different names by different peoples, so of the Reason (*Logos*) that orders all things, and of one Providence that also directs powers ordained to serve under her for all [purposes], have different honours and titles been made according to their laws by different [nations].

3. And there are consecrated symbols, some obscure ones and others more plain, guiding the intelligence towards the mysteries of the Gods, [though] not without risk.

4. For some going entirely astray have stepped into superstitions, while others, shunning superstition as a quagmire, have unwittingly fallen into atheism[1] as down a precipice.

LXVIII. 1. Wherefore especially with regard to such things, should we, taking with us Reason (*Logos*) as our mystic guide out of philosophy, reverently meditate upon each of the things said and done; in order that, [we may avoid what] Theodorus said, [namely] that when he offered his words with his right hand some of his hearers took them with their left—and so not miss the mark by taking in another sense what laws on offerings and feasts have well ordained.

2. For that all [these things] must be referred to the Reason (*Logos*), we may learn from themselves also.

For on the nineteenth of the first month,[2] when they keep a feast to Hermes, they eat honey and figs, saying when so doing, "Truth is sweet." And the amulet of Isis which the myth says she put round her [neck][3] is, when interpreted, "True Voice".

3. And we should not consider Harpocrates either as an imperfect or infant god, or a [god] of pulse,[4] but as protector and chastener of the babyish and imperfect and inarticulate reason that men have about

---

[1] King again, erroneously in my opinion, refers this to the Christians.
[2] Copt. Thoth—corr. roughly with September.
[3] *Cf.* lxv, 2.   [4] *Cf. ibid.*, 3.

THE MYSTERIES OF ISIS AND OSIRIS

Gods. For which cause he has his finger laid upon his lips as a symbol of reticence and silence.

4. And in the month of Mesorē[1] when they make offerings of pulse, they say: "Tongue [is] fortune; tongue is daimon."

5. And they say that of the trees in Egypt the persea especially has been made sacred to the Goddess, because its fruit resembles a heart and its leaf a tongue.

6. For of all man's natural possessions nothing is more godlike than *logos* [word or reason], and especially that concerning the Gods, nor is there anything that decides more weightily for happiness.

7. Wherefore we commend him who goes down to consult the Oracle here[2] to think religiously and speak reverently. But the many act ridiculously when, after they have in the processions and feasts made proclamation to speak reverently, they subsequently speak and think the most irreverent things about the Gods themselves.

LXIX. 1. What use, then, must one make of those melancholy and laughterless and mournful sacrifices, if it is not right either to omit the rites of custom, or to confound our views about Gods and throw them into confusion with absurd suspicions?

2. Yea, among Greeks, too, many things are done, just about the same time also, similar to those which Egyptians perform in the sacred [rites].

3. For instance, at Athens, the women fast at the Thesmophoria, sitting on the ground. While Bœotians move the palace of Achæa,[3] giving that festival the name of Epachthē [the Grief-bringing], as though Demeter were in grief *(ἄχθει)* on account of the Descent[4] of Korē.

4. And this month is the one for sowing when the Pleiades rise, which Egyptians call Athyr,[5] Greeks Pyanepsiōn, and Bœotians Damatrios.[6]

5. Moreover, Theopompus[7] tells us that the Western peoples[8] consider and name the winter Kronos, the summer Aphrodite, and the spring Persephone; and [say] that all things are born from Kronos and Aphrodite.

---

[1] Copt. Mesōrē—corr. roughly with August.   [2] *Sc.* at Delphi.
[3] A surname of Demeter, by which she was worshipped at Athens by the Gephyræans who had emigrated thither from Bœotia (*Herod.*, v, 61).
[4] *Sc.* into Hades.
[5] Copt. Hathōr—corr. roughly to November, or rather last half of October and first of November. *Cf.* also lvi, 10.
[6] That *is*, the month of Demeter.
[7] Müller, i, 328. T. flourished second half of fourth century B.C.
[8] That is, presumably, the Celts.

6. While the Phrygians, thinking that the God sleeps in winter, and wakes in summer, celebrate in his honour the Orgies of his "Going to sleep" at one time, and at another of his "Waking up"; while the Paphlagonians pretend that he is bound hand and foot and imprisoned in winter, and in spring is set in motion and freed from his bonds.

LXX. 1. And the season of the year suggests that the appearance of mourning is assumed at the hiding away of grains [in the earth]—which the ancients did not consider gods, but gifts of the Gods, indispensable [indeed] if we are to live otherwise than savagely and like the brutes.

2. And at the season when, you know, these [ancients] saw the [fruits] entirely disappearing from the trees and ceasing, and those they had sown themselves still scanty and poor—in scraping away the earth with their hands, and pressing it together again, and depositing [the seed] in uncertainty as to whether it would come up again and have its proper consummation, they used to do many things similar to those who bury and mourn.

3. Then, just as we say that one who buys Plato's books "buys Plato", and that one who presents the creations of Menander "acts Menander", so did they not hesitate to call the gifts and creations of the Gods by the names of the Gods—honouring them and reverencing them by use.

4. But those [who came] after, receiving [these names] like boors and ignorantly misapplying what happens[1] to the fruits to the Gods [themselves], and not merely calling but believing the advent and hiding away of the necessaries [of life] generations and destructions of gods, filled their heads with absurd, indecent, and confused opinions, although they had the absurdity of their unreason before their eyes.

5. Excellent, however, was the view of Xenophanes[2] of Colophon that Egyptians don't mourn if they believe in Gods and don't believe in Gods if they mourn; nay, that it would be ridiculous for them in the same breath to mourn and pray for the seed to appear again, in order that it might again be consumed and mourned for.

LXXI. 1. But such is not really the case; but, while mourning for the grain, they pray the Gods, the authors and givers [of it], to renew it again and make other grow up in the place of that which is consumed.

---

[1] τὰ πάθη—lit., "the passions".
[2] X. flourished about end of sixth and beginning of fifth century B.C.

THE MYSTERIES OF ISIS AND OSIRIS

2. Whence there is an excellent saying among the philosophers, that those who do not learn how to hear names rightly, use things wrongly. Just as those of the Greeks who have not learned or accustomed themselves to call bronzes and pictures and marbles images in honour of the Gods, but [call them] Gods, [and] then make bold to say that Lacharēs stripped Athena, and Dionysius cut off Apollo's golden curls, and that Capitoline Zeus was burnt and perished in the Civil Wars—these without knowing it find themselves drawn into adopting mischievous opinions following [directly] on the [abuse of] names.

3. And this is especially the case of Egyptians with regard to the honours they pay to animals. For in this respect, at any rate, Greeks speak rightly when they consider the dove as the sacred creature of Aphrodite, and the dragon of Athena, and the raven of Apollo, and the dog of Artemis, as Euripides [sings]:

Thou shalt be dog, pet of torch-bearing Hecate.[1]

4. Whereas most of the Egyptians, by the service and cult they pay to the animals themselves as though they were Gods, have not only covered their sacred rites entirely with laughter and ridicule—which is the least evil of their fatuity; but a dangerous way of thinking grows up which perverts the weak and simple to pure superstition, and, in the case of the shrewder and bolder, degenerates into an atheistic and brutal rationalism.

5. Wherefore, also, it is not unfitting to run through the conjectures about these things.[2]

CONCERNING THE WORSHIP OF ANIMALS, AND TOTEMISM

LXXII. 1. As for the [theory] that the Gods out of fear of Typhon changed themselves into these animals—as it were hiding themselves in the bodies of ibises and dogs and hawks—it beats any juggling or story-telling.

---

[1] Nauck, p. 525.
[2] Dr Budge (*op. cit.*, i, 29) writes: "Such monuments and texts as we have ... seem to show that the Egyptians first worshipped animals as animals, and nothing more, and later as the habitations of divine spirits and gods; but there is no reason for thinking that the animal worship of the Egyptians was descended from a system of totems and fetishes as Mr J. F. McLennan (*Fortnightly Review*, 1869-1870) believed." I believe myself that the Egyptian animal-cult depended chiefly on the fact that life flowed differently in different animal forms, corresponding with the life-currents in the invisible forms or aspects of the Animal-Soul of the Cosmos.

2. Also the [theory] that all the souls of the dead that persist, have their rebirth[1] into these [animals] only, is equally incredible.

3. And of those who would assign some reason connected with the art of government, some say that Osiris upon his great campaign,[2] divided his force into many divisions—(they call them companies and squadrons in Greek)—and gave them all ensigns of animal figures, and that each of these became sacred and venerated by the clan of those banded together under it.

4. Others [say] that the kings after [Osiris], in order to strike terror into their foes, used to appear dressed in wild beasts' heads of gold and silver.

5. While others tell us that one of the clever and crafty kings, on learning that, though the Egyptians were fickle by nature and quick for change and innovation, they nevertheless possessed an invincible and unrestrainable might owing to their numbers when in agreement and co-operation, showed them and implanted into their minds an enduring superstition—an occasion of unceasing disagreement.

6. For in as much as the beasts—some of which he enacted some [clans] should honour and venerate and others others—are hostile and inimical to one another, and as each one of them by nature likes different food from the others, each [clan] in protecting its own special [beasts] and growing angry at their being injured, was for ever unconsciously being drawn into the enmities of the beasts, and [so] brought into a state of warfare with the others.

7. For even unto this day the people of Wolf-town are the only Egyptians who eat sheep, because the wolf, whom they regard as god, [does so].

8. And the people of Oxyrhynchus-town, in our own day, when the folk of Dog-town ate the oxyrhynchus[3] fish, caught a dog and sacrificing it as a sacred victim, ate it; and going to war because of this, they handled one another roughly, and subsequently were roughly handled by the Romans in punishment.

LXXIII. 1. Again, as many say that the soul of Typhon himself was parted among these animals, the myths would seem enigmatically to hint that every irrational and brutal nature is born from a part of the Evil Daimon, and that to appease and soothe him they pay cult and service to them.

2. But if he fall upon them mighty and dire, bringing on them

---

[1] παλιγγενεσίαν.   [2] *Sc.* for civilising the world.   [3] Lit., "sharp-snout".

THE MYSTERIES OF ISIS AND OSIRIS

excessive droughts, or pestilent diseases, or other unlooked-for strange mischances, then the priests lead away at dark in silence quietly some of the venerated [beasts], and threaten and try to scare away the first [one] of them; if, however, it stops, they consecrate and sacrifice it, as though, I suppose, this were some kind of chastisement of the Daimon, or some specially great means of purification in the greater [emergencies].

3. For in the Goddess-of-child-bed-town[1] they used to burn living men to ashes, as Manethōs has told us, calling them Typhoneian; and the ashes they winnowed away and scattered.[2]

4. This, however, was done publicly, and at one special time, in the Dog-days; whereas the consecratings of the venerated beasts, which are never spoken of and take place at irregular times, according to the emergencies, are unknown to the multitude, except when they have burials, and [the priests] bringing out some of the others, cast them in [to the grave with them] in the presence of all—in the belief that they annoy Typhon in return and curtail what gives him pleasure. For only the Apis and a few other [animals] seem to be sacred to Osiris; while they assign the majority to him [Typhon].

5. And if he [Osiris] is really Reason (*Logos*), I think that the object of our enquiry is found in the case of these [animals] that are admitted to have common honours with him—as, for instance, the ibis, and hawk, and dog-headed ape; [while] Apis himself [is his soul . . .],[3] for thus, you know, they call the goat at Mendes.

LXXIV. 1. There remain of course the utilitarian and symbolical [reasons], of which some have to do with one of the two [Gods], but most [of them] with both.

2. As for the ox and sheep and ichneumon,[4] it is clear they paid them honours on account of their usefulness and utility—just as Lemnians crested larks which seek out and break the eggs of locusts, and Thessalians storks, because when their land produced multitudes of snakes, they came and destroyed them all—(wherefore they made a law that whoever killed a stork should be banished)[5]—so with the asp and weasel and scarab, because they discerned in them certain faint likenesses of the power of the Gods, as it were [that] of the sun in water-drops.

---

[1] ἐν εἰλειθυίας πόλει.   [2] Over the fields?
[3] A *lacuna* occurs here which I have partially filled up, conjecturally, as above.
[4] An Egyptian animal of the weasel kind which was said to hunt out crocodiles' eggs; also called "Pharaoh's rat".
[5] *Cf.* Arist., *Mirab.*, xxiii.

3. For as to the weasel, many still think and say that as it is impregnated through the ear and brings forth by the mouth, it is a likeness of the birth of reason (*logos*).[1]

4. Again [they say] the species of scarab has no female, but all, as males, discharge their seed into the stuff they have made into balls,[2] which they roll along by pushing, moving [themselves] in the opposite direction, just as the sun seems to turn the heaven round in the opposite direction, while it is [the heaven] itself that moves from west to east.[3]

5. And the asp, because it does not age, and moves without limbs with ease and pliancy, they likened to a star.

LXXV. 1. Nay, not even has the crocodile had honour paid it without some show of credible cause, for it alone is tongue-less.[4]

For the Divine Reason (*Logos*) stands not in need of voice, and:

"Moving on a soundless path with justice guides [all] mortal things."[5]

2. And they say that it alone, when it is in the water, has its eyes covered by a smooth and transparent membrane that comes down from the upper lid,[6] so that they see without being seen—an attribute of the First God.[7]

3. And whenever the female lays her eggs on the land, it is known that this will be the limit of the Nile's increase. For as they cannot lay in the water, and fear to do so far from it, they so accurately fore-feel what will be, that they make use of the rise of the river for laying their eggs and hatching them, and yet keep them dry and beyond the danger of being wetted.

[1] *Cf.* xxii, 1—"Physiologus" again. For a criticism of this legend, see R. 43.
[2] *Cf.* x, 9.
[3] Budge (*op. cit.*, ii, 379 f.) writes: "The beetle or scarabæus ... belongs to the family called Scarabacidæ (Coprophagi), of which the *Scarabæus sacer* is the type. ... A remarkable peculiarity exists in the structure and situation of the hind legs, which are placed so near the extremity of the body, and so far from each other as to give the insect a most extraordinary appearance when walking. This peculiar formation is, nevertheless, particularly serviceable to its possessors in rolling the balls of excrementitious matter in which they enclose their eggs. ... These balls are at first irregular and soft, but, by degrees, and during the process of rolling along, become rounder and harder; they are propelled by means of the hind legs. Sometimes these balls are an inch and a half, or two inches in diameter, and in rolling this along the beetles stand almost upon their heads, with the heads turned from the balls." The scarabæus was called *kheprerà* in Egyptian, and was the symbol of *Kheperà* the Great God of creation and resurrection; he was the "father of the gods", and the creator of all things in heaven and earth, self-begotten and self-born; he was usually identified with the rising sun and new-birth generally.
[4] "Physiologus" again, doubtless; it might, however, be said that its tongue is rudimentary.
[5] Euripides, *Tro.*, 887. [6] Lit., "brow". [7] That is, the First-born Reason.

THE MYSTERIES OF ISIS AND OSIRIS

4. And they lay sixty [eggs] and hatch them out in as many days, and the longest-lived of them live as many years—which is the first of the measures for those who treat systematically of celestial [phenomena].[1]

5. Moreover, of those that have honours paid them for both [reasons][2]—of the dog, we have already treated above.[3]

6. As for the ibis, while killing the death-dealing of the reptiles,[4] it was the first to teach them the use of medicinal evacuation, when they observed it being thus rinsed out and purged by itself.[5]

7. While those of the priests who are most punctilious in their observances, in purifying themselves, take the water for cleansing from a place where the ibis has drunk; for it neither drinks unwholesome or poisoned[6] water, nor [even] goes near it.

8. Again, by the relative position of its legs to one another, and [of these] to its beak, it forms an equilateral triangle; and yet again, the variegation and admixture of its black with its white feathers suggest the gibbous moon.[7]

9. Nor ought we to be surprised at Egyptians being so fond of meagre likenesses; for Greeks too in both their pictured and plastic resemblances of Gods use many such [vague indications].

10. For instance, in Crete there was a statue of Zeus which had no ears—for it behoves the Ruler and Lord of all to listen to no one.

11. And Pheidias used the serpent in the [statue] of Athena, and the tortoise in that of Aphrodite at Elis—because on the one hand virgins need protecting, and on the other because keeping-at-home and silence are becoming to married women.

12. Again, the trident of Poseidon is a symbol of the third region, which the sea occupies, assigned [to him] after the heaven and air. For which cause also they invented the names Amphi-trite and Trit-ons.[8]

13. And the Pythagoreans have embellished both numbers and figures with appellations of Gods.

For they used to call the equilateral triangle Athena—Head-born

---

[1] That is, presumably, either the 60 of the Chaldæans, or the $3 \times 4 \times 5$ of the "most perfect" triangle of the Mathematici.
[2] Namely, the utilitarian and symbolical; cf. lxxiv, 1.
[3] Cf. xiv, 6.
[4] Cf. Rawlinson's *Herodotus*, ii, 124, 125.
[5] There is a similar legend in India, I am told.
[6] May also mean "bewitched".
[7] That is, the moon in its third quarter.
[8] From τριτός, "third".

and Third-born[1]—because it is divided by three plumb-lines[2] drawn from the three angles.

14. And [they called] "one" Apollo, from privation of multitude,[3] and owing to the singleness[4] of the monad; and "two" Strife and Daring, and "three" Justice [or Rightness]—for as wronging and being wronged were according to deficiency and excess, rightness [or justice] was born to equality between them.[5]

15. And what is called the Tetraktys, the six-and-thirty, was [their] greatest oath (as has been said over and over again), and is called Cosmos—which is produced by adding together the first four even and [the first] four odd [numbers].[6]

LXXVI. 1. If, then, the most approved of the philosophers, when they perceived in soulless and bodiless things a riddle of the Divine, did not think it right to neglect anything or treat it with disrespect, still more liking, I think, we should then have for the peculiarities in natures that are endowed with sense and possess soul and passion and character—not paying honour to these, but through them to the Divine; so that since they are made by Nature into mirrors clearer [than any man can make], we should consider this as the instrument and art of God who ever orders all things.

2. And, generally, we should deem that nothing soulless is superior to a thing with soul, nor one without sense to one possessing it; not even if one should bring together into one spot all the gold and emeralds in the world.

3. For that which is Divine does not reside in colours or shapes or smoothnesses; nay, all things that either have no share or are not of a nature to share in life, have a lot of less value than that of dead bodies.[7]

4. Whereas the Nature that lives and sees, and has its source of

---

[1] κορυφαγεννῆ καὶ τριτογένειαν,—that is, Koryphagennēs and Tritogeneia.

[2] τρισὶ καθέτοις,—a κάθετος (sc. γραμμή) is generally a perpendicular; but here the reference must be to this appended figure:

△.

[3] That is, presumably, ἀ-πόλλων, from ἀ (priv.) and πολλοί (many).
[4] δι' ἁπλότητα,—the play being apparently ἀ-πολ (πλο)-της.
[5] Lit., in the midst.
[6] The Tetraktys was ordinarily considered to be the sum of the first four numbers simply, that is $1+2+3+4 = 10$; but here we have it given as $1+3+5+7 = 16$, and $2+4+6+8 = 20$, and $16+20 = 36$. The oath is said to have been: "Yea, by Him who did bestow upon our soul Tetraktys, Ever-flowing Nature, Source possessing roots"—the "roots" being the four elements.
[7] Sc. which have at least been the vehicle of life.

THE MYSTERIES OF ISIS AND OSIRIS

motion from itself, and knowledge of things that are its and those that are not, has appropriated both an "efflux of the Good",[1] and a share of the Thinker "by whom the universe is steered", as Heracleitus says.[2]

5. For which cause the Divine is not less well pourtrayed in these [*sc.* animals] than by means of works of art in bronze and stone, which while equally susceptible of decay and mutilations,[3] are in their nature destitute of all feeling and understanding.

6. With regard to the honours paid to animals, then, I approve this view more highly than any other that has been mentioned.

CONCERNING THE SACRED ROBES

LXXVII. 1. Now as to robes: those of Isis [are] variegated in their dyes, for her power [is] connected with matters producing all things and receiving [all]—light darkness, day night, fire water, life death, beginning end; while the [robe] of Osiris has neither shade nor variegation, but one single [property]—the light-like,[4] for the Source is pure and the First and Intelligible unmixed.

2. Wherefore when they have once and once only received this [robe],[5] they treasure it away and keep it from all eyes and hands; whereas they use those of Isis on many occasions.

3. For it is by use that the things which are sensible and ready to hand, present many unfoldings and views of themselves as they change now one way now another; whereas the intelligence of the Intelligible and Pure and Single, shining through the soul, like lightning-flash, once and once only perchance allows [us] to contact and behold [It].

4. For which cause both Plato[6] and Aristotle call this part of philosophy "epoptic",[7] from the fact that they who transcend by the reason (*logos*) these mixed and multiform things of opinion, are raised unto that Primal [One], Simple and Matter-less, and [so] contacting in its singleness the pure truth concerning It, they think philosophy has as it were [its] perfect end.

---

[1] Plat., *Phædr.*, 251 B.
[2] Mullach, i, 328. [3] Reading πηρώσεις.
[4] τὸ φωτοειδές. *Cf.* the better-known term τὸ αὐγοειδές, "the ray-like" (*augoeides*).
[5] Presumably in the initiation symbolising the investiture with the Robe of Glory.
[6] *Symp.*, 210 A.
[7] In its highest sense—that is, intelligible or spiritual "seership", not the symbolic "sight" in the formal Greater Mysteries.

LXXVIII. 1. The fact, moreover, which the present priests cautiously hint at by expiatory sacrifices and covering their faces—[namely] that this God is ruler and king of the dead, being no other than him who is called Hades and Pluto among Greeks—in that they do not know how it is true, confuses the multitude, who suppose that the truly sacred and holy Osiris lives on earth and under earth, where the bodies of those who seem to have [reached their] end are hidden [away].

2. But He Himself is far, far from the earth, unspotted and unstained, and pure of every essence that is susceptible of death and of decay. Nor can the souls of men here [on the earth], swathed as they are with bodies and enwrapped in passions, commune with God, except so far as they can reach some dim sort of a dream [of Him], with the perception of a mind trained in philosophy.

3. But when [their souls] freed [from these bonds] pass to the Formless and Invisible and Passionless and Pure, this God becomes their guide and king, as though they hung on Him, and gazed insatiate upon His Beauty, and longed after it—[Beauty] that no man can declare or speak about.

4. It is with this the ancient tale (*logos*) makes Isis e'er in love, and, by pursuit [of it], and consort [with it], makes [her] full-fill all things down here with all things fair and good, whatever things have part in genesis.

5. Thus, then, these things contain the reason (*logos*) that's more suitable to God.

CONCERNING INCENSE

LXXIX. 1. And must I also speak of the daily incense-offerings, as I promised,[1] the reader should first of all have in mind the fact, that not only have men [in general] always paid most serious attention to things that conduce to health, but that especially in sacred ceremonies and purifications and prescribed modes of life "healthy" is not less important than "holy"; for they did not think it right to render service to the Pure and perfectly Harmless and Unpolluted with either bodies or with souls festering and diseased.

2. Since, then, the air—of which we make most use, and with which we have most to do—does not always keep the same disposition and blend, but at night is condensed, and weighs down the

---

[1] *Cf.* lii, 5.

body, and brings the soul into a desponding and anxious state, as though it had become mist-like and heavy; [therefore] as soon as they get up they incense with pine resin, sanifying and purifying the air by its[1] disintegration, and fanning up again the [fire of the] spirit connate with body[2] which had died down—since its perfume possesses a vehement and penetrating [force].

3. And, again, at midday, perceiving that the sun draws from the earth by force an exceedingly large and heavy exhalation, and commingles it with the air, they incense with myrrh.[3] For its heat dissolves and disperses the turbid and mud-like combination in the atmosphere.

4. And, indeed, physicians seem to relieve sufferers from plague by making a great blaze, as though it cleared the air. But it clears it better if they burn fragrant woods, such as [those] of cypress, juniper, and pine.

5. At any rate, they say that at Athens, at the time of the Great Plague, Akrōn the physician became famous through ordering them to keep fires burning by the side of the sick, for he [thus] benefited not a few.

6. And Aristotle says that the sweet-smelling odours, given off by perfumes and flowers and meadows, conduce no less to health than to enjoyment; because by their warmth and softness they diffuse themselves gently through the brain, which is naturally cold and as though congested.

7. And if, moreover, they call myrrh *bal* among Egyptians—and in translation this comes pretty near to meaning the dispersion of silly talk—this also affords some evidence for the reason why [they use it].

LXXX. 1. And [finally] *kuphi*[4] is a mixture composed of sixteen ingredients: of honey, and wine, and raisins, and cypērus;[5] of pine-resin, and myrrh, and aspalathus,[6] and seseli;[7] and further of mastich,[8]

---

[1] *Sc.* the resin's.
[2] That is, presumably, what was called the "bodily or animal spirits"—the ethers or *prāna's*.
[3] The resinous gum of an Arabian tree; probably a kind of acacia.
[4] This was also used as a medicine.
[5] κυπείρου,—*Cyperus comosus*, an aromatic plant used in embalming, a sweet-smelling marsh plant. *Cf.* F. *cypère* and E. *cypres*.
[6] ἀσπαλάθου,—a prickly shrub yielding a fragrant oil; mentioned in the Apocrypha and in some old herbalists. *Cf.* "I gave a sweet smell like cinnamon and aspalathus"—Ecclus. xxiv, 15. It was not the *Genista acanthoclada*.
[7] σεσέλεως—the *Tordylium officinale*; formerly called in English also "cicely".
[8] σχίνου—or may be "squill".

and bitumen,[1] and nightshade,[2] and sorrel; and in addition to these of both junipers[3] (of which they call the one the larger and the other the smaller), and cardamum, and sweet-flag.[4]

2. And these are not compounded in a haphazard way, but with the sacred writings being read aloud[5] to the perfume-makers when they mix them.

3. And as to their number—even though it has all the appearance of square from square, and [that too] the only one of equally equal numbers that has the power of making the perimeter equal to the area,[6] it must be said that its serviceableness for this purpose at least is of the slightest.

4. But the majority of the ingredients, as they possess aromatic properties, liberate a sweet breath and healthy exhalation, by which both the air is changed, and the body being gently and softly moved by the vapour, falls asleep[7] and loosens the distressing strain of the day's anxieties, as though they were knots, [and yet] without any intoxication.

5. Moreover, they polish up the image-making and receptive organ of dreams like a mirror, and make it clearer, no less than the playing on the lyre which the Pythagoreans used to use before sleep, thus charming away and sanifying the passionate and reason-less nature of the soul.

6. For things smelt call back the failing sense, and often, on the other hand, dull and quiet it by [their] soothing [effect], when their exhalations are diffused through the body; just as some of the physicians say that sleep is induced when the vaporisation of the food, as it were creeping gently round the inward parts and groping about, produces a kind of tickling.

7. And they use *kuphi* both as draught and mixture; for when it is drunk it is thought to purge the intestines, [but when applied externally[8]] to be an emollient.

8. And apart from these [considerations], resin is a work of the sun; and myrrh [comes from] the exudation of the trees under the

---

[1] ἀσφάλτου.
[2] θρύου—or may be "rush".
[3] Lit., juniper-berries.
[4] κάλαμου—probably *Acorus calamus* (*cf.* Ex. xxx, 23 *et al.*). It is to be noticed that the ingredients are arranged in four sets of four each.
[5] That is to the sound of *mantrāḥ*, as a Hindu would say.
[6] *Cf.* xlii, 2, and figure in note.
[7] The *kuphi* being used at sundown.
[8] A *lacuna* of 8 or 9 letters occurs here in E.

sun-heat; while of the ingredients of *kuphi*, some flourish more at night, like all things whose nature it is to be nourished by cool breezes and shade and dew and damp.

9. Seeing that the light of day is one and single, and Pindar tells us that the sun is seen "through empty æther";[1] while air is a blend and mixture of many lights and properties, as it were of seeds dropped from every star into one [field].

10. Naturally, then, they use the former as incenses by day, as being single and having their birth from the sun; and the latter when night sets in, as being mixed and manifold in its qualities.

AFTERWORD

So ends this exceedingly instructive treatise of Plutarch, which, in spite of the mass of texts and monuments concerning Àsàr and Àst which have already been deciphered by the industry of Egyptologists, remains the most complete account of the root mystery-myth of ancient Egypt. The myth of Osiris and Isis goes back to the earliest times of which we have record, and is always found in the same form. Indeed the "Ritual", the "Book of the Dead", which should rather be called the "Book of the Living", might very well be styled "The Gospel of Osiris".

It would be out of place here to seek for the historical origin of this Great Mystery; certainly Osiris was originally something greater than a "water sprite", as Budge supposes. Osiris and Isis were and are *originally*, as I believe, cosmic or super-cosmic beings; for the Elder and Younger Horus, regarded macrocosmically, were the Intelligible and Sensible Worlds, and, regarded microcosmically, pertained to the mystery of the Christ-stage of manhood.

It may, of course, be denied that the ancient Egyptians were capable of entertaining any such notions; we, however, prefer the tradition of our Trismegistic tractates to the "primitive-culture" theories of anthropological speculation. That, however, such views were entertained in the first centuries is incontrovertible, as may be seen from a careful study of Philo of Alexandria alone. Thus to quote one passage out of many with regard to the two Horoi:

"For that *this* cosmos is the Younger Son of God, in that it is perceptible to sense. The Son who's older than this one, He hath declared to be no one [perceptible by sense], for that he is conceivable

[1] *Olymp.*, i, 6.

by mind alone. But having judged him worthy of the Elder's rights, He hath determined that he should remain with Him alone."[1]

When, moreover, we speak of the Christ-stage of manhood, we mean all that mystery that lies beyond the normal stage of man, including both the super-man stage and that of the Christ.

In any case, Plutarch is of the greatest service for understanding the atmosphere and environment in which the students of the Trismegistic tradition moved, and we have therefore bestowed more care upon him than perhaps the general reader may think necessary.

[1] *Quod Deus Im.*, § 6; M. 1, 277, P. 298 (Ri. ii, 72, 73).

This is the end of this publication.

Any remaining blank pages are for our book binding requirements and are blank on purpose.

To search thousands of interesting publications like this one, please remember to visit our website at:

http://www.kessinger.net